BIBLE 101

FROM **GENESIS** AND **PSALMS** TO **THE GOSPELS** AND **REVELATION,** YOUR GUIDE TO THE **OLD** AND **NEW TESTAMENTS**

Edward D. Gravely, PhD, and Peter Link Jr., PhD

ADAMS MEDIA

NEW YORK   LONDON   TORONTO   SYDNEY   NEW DELHI

Adams Media
An Imprint of Simon & Schuster, Inc.
100 Technology Center Drive
Stoughton, Massachusetts 02072

First Adams Media hardcover edition January 2023

ADAMS MEDIA and colophon are trademarks of Simon & Schuster.

For information about special discounts for bulk purchases, please contact Simon & Schuster Special Sales at 1-866-506-1949 or business@simonandschuster.com.

The Simon & Schuster Speakers Bureau can bring authors to your live event. For more information or to book an event contact the Simon & Schuster Speakers Bureau at 1-866-248-3049 or visit our website at www.simonspeakers.com.

Manufactured in the United States of America

10 9 8 7 6 5 4 3 2

Library of Congress Cataloging-in-Publication Data
Names: Gravely, Edward D., author. | Link, Peter (Peter Jackson) Jr., author.
Title: Bible 101 / Edward D. Gravely, PhD, and Peter Link Jr., PhD.
Description: First Adams Media hardcover edition. | Stoughton, Massachusetts: Adams Media, 2023. | Series: 101 series | Includes index.
Identifiers: LCCN 2022037402 | ISBN 9781507219805 (hc) | ISBN 9781507219812 (ebook)
Subjects: LCSH: Bible--Introductions.
Classification: LCC BS475.3 .G73 2023 | DDC 220.6/1--dc23/eng/20220908
LC record available at https://lccn.loc.gov/2022037402

ISBN 978-1-5072-1980-5
ISBN 978-1-5072-1981-2 (ebook)

CONTENTS

INTRODUCTION 7

WHAT IS THE BIBLE?. 9

THE LANGUAGE, STRUCTURE, AND ORGANIZATION
OF MODERN BIBLES 14

HOW THE OLD TESTAMENT AND NEW TESTAMENT
RELATE TO EACH OTHER. 20

OLD TESTAMENT BASICS. 25

THE TORAH, AN OVERVIEW 32

GENESIS 1–11. 37

GENESIS 12–50 41

EXODUS 1–18. 46

EXODUS 19–40. 51

LEVITICUS 56

NUMBERS 61

DEUTERONOMY 65

THE PROPHETS, AN OVERVIEW 69

JOSHUA. 73

JUDGES. 78

1 SAMUEL 83

2 SAMUEL 87

1 KINGS. 91

2 KINGS. 96

ISAIAH. 101

JEREMIAH 106

EZEKIEL. 111

THE TWELVE MINOR PROPHETS, PART 1. 116

THE TWELVE MINOR PROPHETS, PART 2. 121

THE TWELVE MINOR PROPHETS, PART 3. 126

THE WRITINGS, AN OVERVIEW. 131

PSALMS. 135

JOB. 139

PROVERBS. 144

RUTH AND SONG OF SOLOMON
(OR SONG OF SONGS). 149

ECCLESIASTES AND LAMENTATIONS 153

ESTHER. 157

DANIEL 161

EZRA. 166

NEHEMIAH 170

1 AND 2 CHRONICLES. 175

NEW TESTAMENT BASICS 179

THE FOUR GOSPELS. 184

THE GOSPEL OF MATTHEW 189

THE GOSPEL OF MARK 194

THE GOSPEL OF LUKE. 198

THE GOSPEL OF JOHN 202

ACTS. 206

PAUL AND HIS TRAVELS 210

ROMANS 215

1–2 CORINTHIANS 220

GALATIANS 224

EPHESIANS 229

PHILIPPIANS 233

COLOSSIANS 237

1–2 THESSALONIANS .241

1–2 TIMOTHY AND TITUS 245

PHILEMON 249

HEBREWS 253

JAMES 257

1 PETER 261

2 PETER AND JUDE 265

1–3 JOHN 269

REVELATION 274

THE BIBLE TODAY 279

INDEX 282

INTRODUCTION

Perhaps the best-known book of all time, the Bible is a beloved text the world over. It tells one grand story of God's love for humankind in many different ways, including moral teachings, sacred stories, and classic doctrines that have endured for thousands of years. But reading the Bible can be overwhelming at times—there are perplexing words and phrases, countless important figures, and locations that may be unfamiliar to modern readers. *Bible 101* simplifies the process for you with easy-to-read summaries of all the key parts.

Whether you've been studying the Bible for years or are newly interested, *Bible 101* will help you better understand its people, lessons, and teachings. You'll find important historical context and background, learn about the principal authors of the Bible, and better appreciate the meaning of the many parables and stories. Reading this book as a companion to your Bible will ensure you understand important chapters and verses. As you read through each section, you'll become familiar with key biblical moments, including:

- How God created the world, explained in Genesis
- God's covenant of laws, revealed in Exodus
- The poetic story of how God will redeem His people, told in the book of Psalms
- The theological history of the life, death, and resurrection of Jesus, detailed in the Gospel of Matthew

- The story of the early days of the Christian church, described in the book of Acts
- One of the earliest records of Christian thinking about the philosophies and religions of the ancient world, outlined in Colossians

Whether you're reading the word of God as a source of spiritual fulfillment, moral teachings, or historical knowledge, you'll find explanations, inspiration, and analysis in *Bible 101*. Get ready to dive into—and truly understand—all the trials and triumphs in this captivating volume.

WHAT IS THE BIBLE?

The World's Most Popular Book

"Thy word is a lamp unto my feet, and a light unto my path."
—Psalms 119:105

At its most basic, the Bible is a collection of religious texts that are considered sacred Scripture primarily by Christians and Jewish people. The Bible's message about God, His people, and salvation has endured for millennia to become *the* book that guides the lives of billions of human beings on planet Earth.

A DESCRIPTION OF THE BIBLE

The Bible is made up of two major sections: Christians call them the *Old Testament* and the *New Testament*. Jewish people recognize only the first section (the Old Testament) as sacred Scripture, and they call it the *Tanakh*. After some early Jewish people came to believe that Jesus of Nazareth, a Jewish man, was the Savior Messiah that was promised in the Tanakh, they came to recognize the writings of Jesus' original disciples as Scripture as well, and thus the New Testament was born.

The Origin of the Word *Tanakh*

The word *Tanakh* (sometimes spelled *Tanak*) is an acronym for the three parts of the Jewish Scripture in Hebrew: the Law (the Torah), the Prophets (the

Nevi'im), and the Writings (the Ketuvim)—TNK (Tanakh). The word *testament* in the context of the Bible means "covenant." Christians, what the followers of Jesus of Nazareth came to be called, saw what is now called the New Testament as the fulfillment of the covenants God made in the Old Testament, and named the testaments accordingly. Christianity quickly spread beyond the ethnic borders of Judaism, and the New Testament spread with it.

There are thirty-nine books in the Old Testament and twenty-seven books in the New Testament, for a total of sixty-six different books, or texts. Though the contents of the Old Testament have remained constant for millennia, various editions of the Old Testament have not always counted the books the same way, nor have the books always been presented in the same order. Some ancient sources claim as few as twenty-two books in the Old Testament, but they are not missing any books. Rather, they are counting the books differently. For example, 1–2 Samuel in modern Bibles is two books, but is simply Samuel (one book) in the Tanakh, and what modern Bibles list as the twelve minor prophets (*minor* for their length, not their significance) were often included as one book, the Book of the Twelve in ancient Hebrew Bibles.

What Does the Word *Bible* Mean?

The English word *Bible* comes from a Greek word that means "the books" (*ta biblia*). The term appears to have originated among Greek-speaking Jewish people to refer to the Tanakh. The first Christian use of this term to describe both the Old and New Testaments was in the late fourth century.

The Bible is very old, though its exact date is unknown. There is still much debate about the topic. Scholars currently estimate that the writing of the Old Testament began between 2,800 and 3,400 years ago, and the whole Bible was finished close to 2,000 years ago, shortly after the time of Jesus.

WHAT JESUS BELIEVED ABOUT THE BIBLE

Christians have inherited their understanding of the Old Testament from those earliest Christian Jewish people and from Jesus himself. This book is a Christian approach to the Bible with respect for other traditions, so the opinion of Jesus on the Old Testament will be a very important consideration.

In the New Testament, Jesus often refers to the Old Testament by its constituent parts as the Jewish people in his day understood them: the Law, the Prophets, and the Writings. Jesus quotes frequently from the Old Testament in his teaching, quoting from every major section of the Old Testament.

Jesus believed not only in the historical accuracy of the events described in the Old Testament but also that the Old Testament text was inspired by God Himself. In the New Testament, Jesus speaks as though he clearly believes that Adam and Eve were real people, Jonah really was swallowed by a giant fish, and Noah's flood really happened. When he refers to Old Testament passages, Jesus uses the name of the author ("as Moses said"), the name of the section ("as the Scripture says"), and the word for God ("as God says") interchangeably.

WHAT CHRISTIANS BELIEVE ABOUT THE BIBLE

Taking their cues from Jesus, Christians have historically believed that both the Old and the New Testaments are inspired by God. Though the books do have human authors, God is also the author of the Scripture in a significant way. The term often used to describe this belief is *inspiration*. Though there has been an energetic discussion among Christians throughout the centuries about the method and nature of inspiration, Christians consistently describe the books of the Bible as being inspired by God. They do not mean that God was merely a *source* of inspiration for the writing of the books. They typically mean that the books are the very word of God.

Because Christians believe that the Bible is inspired by God, they also believe that the Bible has great authority in their lives. Though expressions of this authority have taken many forms, most Christians have historically agreed that to disobey the Bible is to disobey God Himself. Consequently, Christians have taken Bible reading and Bible study very seriously.

Where Are the Deuterocanonical Books and the Apocrypha?

The deuterocanonical books and the Apocrypha (both Old and New Testament) have been left out of this book because they are not included in most modern Bibles. There are many high-quality Roman Catholic and Eastern Orthodox treatments of those books available.

The Christian view of inspiration and authority, however, has not led most Christians to ignore the human role in the production of the Bible. For example, Christians have believed that the Gospel of Matthew is God's word and carries with it God's authority. They have also simultaneously believed that the Gospel of Matthew was written from Matthew's perspective, using his knowledge, vocabulary, and culture. Significant debate remains among Christians as to exactly how God did that, but it has been a consistent belief for Christians throughout the centuries.

KEY TAKEAWAYS

The Bible is one book with two testaments, sixty-six books, and dozens of authors. The Tanakh (Old Testament) is the primary sacred text for Jewish people, modern and ancient, and the Old and New Testaments together form the exclusive sacred text for Christians the world over. Like Jesus himself, Christians believe the Bible to be the Word of God and to have ultimate authority in their lives. Knowing the Bible and knowing God Himself are inextricably linked.

THE LANGUAGE, STRUCTURE, AND ORGANIZATION OF MODERN BIBLES

Tools That Make the Bible Easier to Read

"Study to shew thyself approved unto God, a workman that needeth
not to be ashamed, rightly dividing the word of truth."
—2 Timothy 2:15

The Bible is available in many different physical and digital formats and translations. To make the Bible easier to read, modern publishers use tools like abbreviations, section headers, and footnotes to streamline long citations, separate important chunks of text, and explain certain references. These tools can be a little confusing, even though they are there to help you. In this section, you will learn why these tools are there and how they can help make the structure of the Bible clearer.

A VERY BRIEF HISTORY OF THE ENGLISH BIBLE

Originally, the Bible was not available to English-speaking people in Europe. It was available only in Latin, which dramatically limited the access of its contents to most people. Work on translating the Bible into English began as far back as the seventh century.

In 1380, John Wycliffe began translating the entire Bible into Middle English, probably with significant help from his students. The Roman Catholic Church of Wycliffe's day responded with great hostility, condemning any further translation work of the Latin Bible into English and outlawing even the act of reading Wycliffe's translation. What Wycliffe set in motion, however, could not be undone.

William Tyndale completed and published another English translation of the New Testament by 1526, with work on the Old Testament quickly underway. Like Wycliffe, church authorities condemned Tyndale's work from the outset. Tyndale fled from England to Europe to remain safe, but, after producing a revised edition in 1534, he was arrested in Antwerp, tried, and executed for heresy. Within a decade of Tyndale's death, however, a half dozen more Bibles in English were published.

The Legacy of the King James Version

Since its production in 1611, the King James Version has been one of the best-selling books in world history. Even today, with its language hundreds of years out of date, and with many excellent modern English translations available, the KJV is still the preferred Bible of many Christians in English.

In an effort to unify the English Bible tradition for ecclesiastical and political reasons, James I commissioned the production of a new English translation. This was to be a diplomatic translation, produced by scholars, that could be used by all the protestant groups in England. The Authorized Version was published in 1611 and is known today as the King James Version (KJV). The KJV was subsequently revised four times over the next one hundred fifty years, and it is the 1769 revision that is most commonly read today.

VARIOUS BIBLE VERSIONS AND TRANSLATIONS

Bookstore shelves and bookselling websites are filled with Bibles of every brand and price point imaginable. Different modern translations use different verbiage to translate the ancient Greek and Hebrew, but they all say essentially the same thing. The English of the King James Version is centuries old, but most translations currently available were written in the twentieth century and use modern English. Additionally, some modern translations prefer more of a word-for-word approach to translating the original languages of the Bible, while others opt for more of a thought-for-thought translation.

The massive price difference among Bibles is determined almost entirely by what the cover is made of or by how many study notes the book contains. Additionally, most Bible publishers have apps and websites to distribute their modern translations free of charge.

BOOK NAMES AND ABBREVIATIONS

The book names in a modern Bible are anglicized (adapted to English), typically from their ancient Hebrew or Greek names. Because the Bible existed in Latin for a very long time, there is also a Latin influence in what the books are called. The original authors of the

Bible did not provide these book names—they evolved over time into the English forms we have today.

Biblical scholars and centuries of popular usage have produced a reasonably common set of abbreviations for the Bible book names to make them easier to refer to in writing. Though the names are not always abbreviated in exactly the same way, it is usually not difficult to tell which Bible book is being referred to by the letters that are there (for example, the book of Romans is abbreviated as both Rom and Rm by scholars). Throughout this book, both the academic three-letter abbreviations and the full names of the books will be used.

CHAPTERS AND VERSES

The individual books in the Bible are divided into chapters, and each chapter is divided into verses. The original authors of the Bible did not make these divisions. When Matthew wrote Matthew, for example, punctuation *of any kind* was not in widespread use, and writers of Greek were not yet spacing between their words. The chapters, verses, spaces between words, and punctuation were added by later publishers to make the text easier to read.

The chapter divisions in use today are about eight hundred years old, and the verse divisions within those chapters are about five hundred years old. They have been a part of English Bibles since the first English Bibles began to appear, but they do not necessarily reflect the logic or rhetoric of the original authors. The chapters and verses appear to have been created solely for logistical support—in other words, they make it easier to find paragraphs and sentences within the Bible; they do little to help readers understand the meaning of the text.

When writing the reference for a passage of Scripture, the common convention is to give the book title, chapter number, and verse number(s), with a colon separating the two numbers (e.g., Genesis 3:16). This example would be read as "Genesis three sixteen." For another example, "Matthew six thirty-three" indicates the book of Matthew, Chapter 6, verse 33, written "Matthew 6:33." When writers and speakers wish to refer to an entire chapter, they simply leave off the verse designation, so "Matthew 3" refers to Chapter 3 of Matthew as a whole.

A few books in the Bible are so short they do not have chapters, only verses. They are, in effect, a single chapter. Locations in these books are referred to by verse only. So, the sixth verse in the book of Jude is referred to simply as "Jude 6."

SECTION HEADERS, MARGINAL NOTES, AND FOOTNOTES

In addition to chapters and verses, most modern Bibles employ section headers and paragraphs to break up the text and to make passages easy to find. In Matthew 4, for example, most modern Bibles have verses 1–11 as a single paragraph with some sort of heading that indicates this section of text is about the temptation of Jesus. Before verse 12 begins, most modern Bibles have a heading that indicates the following text discusses the beginning of Jesus' ministry. Just like the chapters and verses, these were not originally part of the Bible. They were added much later to make the Bible easier to read.

Modern Bibles—largely print versions—also have a host of marginal notes and footnotes for the interested Bible student. The marginal notes frequently refer the reader to other places in the Bible where a similar concept or theme occurs. When a Bible passage quotes another place in Scripture (which happens with great frequency), the marginal notes indicate the source of the quote. For example, in the New Testament, Mark opens his Gospel with two quotes from the Old Testament (Mark 1:2–3). The marginal notes in most printed Bibles identify that the first quote comes from Malachi 3:1 and the second comes from Isaiah 40:3.

Footnotes are often reserved for explanations about what words mean if the meaning is not obvious in English. Footnotes can also explain a theological concept or discuss how some other ancient manuscripts of the Bible might read differently if the ancient manuscripts are not all exactly alike at a particular place. Some modern Bibles are dubbed "study Bibles" because they have extensive introductory notes, footnotes, and articles throughout to clarify the meaning of the text.

Again, none of these notes were written by the original authors of the Bible; they were added by modern-day editors and printers to make Bible reading easier.

KEY TAKEAWAYS

Throughout recent centuries, Christians have been working hard to make the Bible easier to read and more accessible to new readers. Chapters, verses, headings, marginal notes, footnotes, and study Bibles break up the text of this very long book and help explain its concepts. No matter what your reasons for reading the Bible, you can surely find an edition that's right for you.

HOW THE OLD TESTAMENT AND NEW TESTAMENT RELATE TO EACH OTHER

Reading the Bible As One Book

> "Search the scriptures; for in them ye think ye have eternal life:
> and they are they which testify of me."
> —John 5:39

All Christians affirm both the Old Testament and the New Testament as Scripture. There has never been a time when the church did not have the Old Testament as its Bible or as the first part of its Bible. Various Christian traditions, however, have understood differently how the Old Testament and New Testament relate to each other. What are some of the questions surrounding how the two testaments form one Bible? How do the two parts form one Bible that is both coherent and cohesive?

IMPORTANT DIFFERENCES BETWEEN THE OLD AND NEW TESTAMENTS

There are two obvious differences between the Old Testament and the New: different languages and different time periods. First, the Old Testament is primarily written in Biblical Hebrew with a little bit of Biblical Aramaic. The New Testament, however, is written in

Koine Greek, which was the common language across the known world at its time. Second, the Old Testament canon finds completion between 400 to 200 B.C. and then is translated into Greek and other languages by the time of Jesus. The New Testament is written over a much shorter period and formed into a book much more quickly.

THE OLD TESTAMENT AS FOUNDATION FOR THE NEW TESTAMENT

The most common approach that Christians follow is to regard the Old Testament as a necessary foundation for the New. Without considering whether the Old Testament's message matches the New, the Old's content and categories prepare for the New Testament in at least two ways:

1. The New Testament provides the next part of the Old's story.
2. The Old Testament offers theological categories the New needs.

First, the Old Testament provides a story whose next "chapter" is continued in the New. The New Testament affirms the Old's storyline. In some sense, most Christians view the New as the Old's "sequel." The Old Testament sets up the New, and the New Testament completes the Old. The Old Testament story offers essential information about Adam and Eve, Abraham, Isaac, Jacob, Moses, David, and the nation Israel for the New, and it promises new days that have yet to come. God's story with Israel is not done in the Old Testament because the reader waits for the Son of David.

Second, the Old Testament provides theological concepts essential to the New. Most importantly, it promises a Messiah through its imagery of the "seed" of the woman; the "seed" of Abraham, Isaac, and Jacob; the king from the tribe of Judah; the Prophet Like Moses; and the Son of David. The New Testament presumes a knowledge of such theological categories, and the Old Testament reader anticipates the need for more theological information. Many theological categories, such as man's sin, sacrifices, atonement, and resurrection, all begin in the Old Testament but are not fully explored because God's promises to Israel and the nations are not yet completed. Perhaps the most common theological category to link the testaments is that of prophecy: Old Testament predictions are fulfilled during the New Testament's events.

The Church's First Sermon

In Acts 2, the Apostle Peter preaches on Pentecost after the Holy Spirit falls upon the disciples. His primary texts are Joel, Psalms, and 2 Samuel 7. Through the sharing of these Old Testament texts, three thousand people became Christians and trusted Jesus as Savior and Lord.

THE NEW TESTAMENT READS THE OLD TESTAMENT ANEW

Most Christians accept these theological categories. Differences emerge, however, when Christians consider how to reconcile apparent or real differences between the two testaments. For most Christians, if debate ensues between the Old and New, the New Testament's perspective prevails. Christians do not always agree on the rationale behind the superiority of the New. For example, some will contend that the New Testament corrects, updates, or replaces the Old. Others will contend that the New Testament clarifies how the Old should have been read all along. No matter the reasoning, most Christians, when pushed into questions of theology or practical living, will answer using material in the New Testament.

There are at least three potential dangers with this approach:

1. Quickly presuming that the New Testament conveys different ideas than the Old may be a misreading of the Old Testament.
2. Not letting the Old Testament's ideas and their presentations stand on their own runs the risk of drawing Christians away from reading the Old Testament, an idea the New Testament explicitly rejects.
3. When Christians minimize their interactions with the Old Testament, the New's depth is also missed because it presumes and emphasizes the Old.

THE OLD TESTAMENT PROCLAIMS THE NEW COVENANT

Because of these concerns and a long history of the church reading the Old Testament as Christian Scripture, some Christians argue that the tensions between the Old and New are matters of misreading the Old. Without relying on the New Testament to refine the Old, such a view seeks to wrestle with the Old on its own terms to see if its message coheres with the New Testament regarding humankind's problems and God's solution. In such a view, the understanding of the Torah in the Prophets and the Writings reflects a reading of the Torah consistent with the New Testament's reading of it. The Old Testament offers the same message as the New, but its setting is different. It describes Israel's failures under the old, Mosaic Covenant to give hope in a man who is coming whose life will offer hope in a new covenant. This view reflects *Bible 101*'s approach because the Old and New Testaments offer hope in approaching God and living in His presence only through God's promised Messiah.

KEY TAKEAWAYS

Christians use different models to understand how the Old Testament and New Testament fit together to make the Bible. The Old Testament is best understood, however, when both Testaments are viewed as sharing the same message communicated in two different settings.

OLD TESTAMENT BASICS

The Old Testament and Its Big Ideas

> "Then began men to call upon the name of the LORD."
> —Genesis 4:26

This section offers a brief overview of the Old Testament. First, you'll learn what the Old Testament is before moving on to investigate its languages and manuscripts. We then examine the Old Testament's contents by considering its different orders so that you can understand how *Bible 101* organizes its layout of the Old Testament. This book handles the Old Testament in one of the Hebrew three-part orders: Torah, Prophets, and Writings. There was more than one way that communities organized the books contained in the Writings. However, it was always a three-part order and the contents of the third part, the Writings, were always the same.

WHAT IS THE OLD TESTAMENT?

The Old Testament is the original and authoritative religious book for both Jewish people and Christians. In Judaism, this book is not known as the Old Testament, but as the Hebrew Bible or by its abbreviated form: Tanakh. Christians bind the Old Testament to the New. Before the New Testament was formed, Christians explained their understanding of God, humans, and salvation from the Old Testament, with an authoritative Old Testament appearing in some form between 400 and 200 B.C.

Multiple factions of Jewish readers scattered across the known world wrestled with how to understand this book, but two primary ways of reading the Old Testament prevailed after Rome's destruction of the temple in A.D. 70: the Pharisees', whose ideas would mature into Judaism, and the Apostles', whose readings and writings would develop Christianity.

THE LANGUAGES OF THE OLD TESTAMENT

The Old Testament was written in dead languages that no one currently speaks, with Biblical Hebrew as the Old Testament's primary language. When Jewish people began returning from their exile in Babylon, Aramaic became the language of those generations. As such, it is not surprising that parts of later Old Testament books were written in this sister language, Biblical Aramaic. Major sections of Daniel and Ezra were written in Biblical Aramaic, and this language also appears in individual phrases and terms in other parts of the Old Testament.

THE MANUSCRIPTS OF THE OLD TESTAMENT

Modern translators of the Old Testament derive their texts from three ancient manuscript families. Along with the New Testament, the Old Testament remains one of the best-attested ancient works of any kind. Unlike most ancient books, there is overwhelming evidence to trust that we have the original form:

1. First, the most reliable and best-preserved manuscripts come from the Masoretic Text family. These Biblical Hebrew manuscripts were copied over centuries by the Masoretes, who were ancient Jewish scribes. Their work is the main evidence for the Old Testament's original form.
2. Second, ancient Greek–speaking Jewish people translated the Old Testament into the common Greek of their day in a version and versions called the *Septuagint*. (The *Septuagint* is referred to as both a single version and as a compilation of multiple versions.)
3. Third, collections of Biblical Hebrew manuscripts known as the Dead Sea Scrolls were found hidden in desert caves, beginning in 1947. These manuscripts replicate much of the Masoretic Text, but at key moments, they show a Hebrew reading consistent with the Septuagint.

Modern English translations follow the Masoretic Text, but they will occasionally differ from it when the Septuagint and Dead Sea Scrolls agree with each other against the Masoretic Text. Modern translators also consult the other two as they determine the original text.

THE ORDER OF THE BOOKS IN THE OLD TESTAMENT

The Old Testament was written and recorded on scrolls. The ancient communities who read the Old Testament ordered these scrolls according to their various ways of reading. The oldest ways of reading reflected a three-part order of the Old Testament rather than the four-part order of English Bibles. The three parts of the Old Testament are Torah, Prophets, and Writings. The English Old Testament's four-part order organizes itself by genre, the kinds of literature: law, history, wisdom and poetry, and prophets.

Various Orders of Chapters in the Old Testament

The Old Testament was written on scrolls and passed from one generation to the next. Each community organized and ordered scrolls according to how they made sense of them. As one generation tried to obey what they read in their scrolls, they influenced the next generations by passing on the text, what it means, and how to read it. How they read the scrolls influenced how they ordered them.

THE BOOKS IN EACH PART OF THE OLD TESTAMENT

Because the three-part order is more likely to be the original order, *Bible 101*'s study of the Old Testament is organized into one version of the three-part order.

The Torah

The Torah represents the first part of the Old Testament. It is a book unto itself: Moses' book. It contains a strategic combination of narrative, poetry, law codes, and genealogies. It is one book made up of other books:

- Genesis
- Exodus
- Leviticus
- Numbers
- Deuteronomy

The Prophets

The second part of the Old Testament is the Prophets. Its beginning emphasizes meditating upon the Torah day and night. This second part of the Old Testament reminds the reader to keep thinking about the Torah.

The Prophets itself divides into two parts: the Former Prophets, a story of the nation of Israel's time in the land of Canaan, and the Latter Prophets, a prophetic reflection on how to read the Former Prophets and the Torah. The Latter Prophets includes three major prophets and twelve minor prophets. These twelve minor prophets form one book together: the Book of the Twelve. The books of the Prophets include:

The Former Prophets (mostly narrative)
- Joshua
- Judges
- 1 Samuel
- 2 Samuel
- 1 Kings
- 2 Kings

The Latter Prophets (mostly prophecy)
- Isaiah
- Jeremiah

- Ezekiel
- The Book of the Twelve (Twelve Minor Prophets)
  - Hosea
  - Joel
  - Amos
  - Obadiah
  - Jonah
  - Micah
  - Nahum
  - Habakkuk
  - Zephaniah
  - Haggai
  - Zechariah
  - Malachi

The Writings

The third part of the Old Testament is the Writings. Just as the Prophets begins with a command to meditate on the Torah day and night, so, too, the Writings begins by describing someone who actually does meditate upon the Torah all the time. By pulling together diverse narratives, prophecy, poetry, and genealogies, this third part of the Old Testament calls the reader to continually think about the Torah. The books of the Writings are:

- Psalms
- Job
- Proverbs
- Ruth
- Song of Solomon (Song of Songs)
- Ecclesiastes

- Lamentations
- Esther
- Daniel
- Ezra
- Nehemiah
- 1 Chronicles
- 2 Chronicles

KEY TAKEAWAYS

The Old Testament begins all Christian and Jewish theological conversations. In *Bible 101*, we examine this ancient conversation that reaches us today in its three-part order of the Torah, the Prophets, and the Writings. It is a book made up of books whose diverse literature, including narratives, poetry, law codes, and genealogies, forms one grand story from the creation of all things until the end of all things. It teaches how God relates to all peoples by His relationship with one people, the nation of Israel, and His promises to them. We have an abundance of ancient manuscripts passed into our modern hands that reinforces our confidence in the accuracy and validity of the Old Testament.

THE TORAH, AN OVERVIEW

God's Instruction

"He is the Rock, his work is perfect: for all his ways are judgment: a God of
truth and without iniquity, just and right is he."
—Deuteronomy 32:4

The Torah is the first part of the Old Testament, and every part of it
connects to its most important event: the nation of Israel's time at
Mount Sinai when God draws close to Israel. In this section, we sum-
marize the Torah's major characters and how they fit into its story,
which begins with God creating all things and ends with the hope
of people from all nations living with God forever through a person
who will come in the last days. The last days are a time when God
will be upon earth.

WHAT IS THE TORAH?

The Torah is one book in five parts that covers God's work from the
beginning of time to its end. Some scholars refer to this book as "the
Pentateuch," which means a fivefold book. It contains five volumes,
or books, that we know in English translations as Genesis, Exodus,
Leviticus, Numbers, and Deuteronomy.

English translations commonly render the term *Torah* as *Law*.
Such a translation explains much of the book, but the term *Torah*
primarily means "instruction." The Torah contains four major
genres: narrative, poetry, law code, and genealogy. It strategically

intertwines these genres to form a majestic tapestry. Every piece has a purpose. Each section gives instruction.

The diversity of genres within the Torah yields a complex book. How readers understand the rhythms of these genres and their relative importance to the book sheds light on how they define the Torah's emphasis. Some readers accentuate the Torah's many law codes because they focus on ethics, teaching how people should live. Others highlight the narratives, because they focus on its history of what God did for Israel and all the nations. Still others stress how the narratives and poetry work together to explain how things will end for humanity (its eschatology). This last approach focuses on the Torah teaching what will happen in the last days based on what God did in the beginning.

The Torah's Genres

The Torah, Genesis through Deuteronomy, is one book, but it employs four primary genres: narrative, poetry, law code, and genealogy. It mixes these genres in discernible patterns that should guide interpretation. For example, narrative sections are followed by poetry that echoes parts of the narrative. In a similar manner, the law codes are surrounded by narratives that show the need for the laws and how the laws never really fix the core problem. The interplay of these genres unveils strategies to teach the Torah's message.

The primary setting of the Torah's story is the nation Israel's life under the Mosaic Covenant, a covenant with laws from God that the nation Israel receives at Mount Sinai. Mount Sinai proves important because God and people briefly come close to living together there when God descends on the mountain. This time at this mountain reminds us how God and man come together in creation, and it previews the future coming together of humanity and God in the last days.

When God draws close to the nation Israel at Mount Sinai, His terrifying presence and Israel's fearful response underscore the peril of human death in God's presence and highlight the need for God's word. The other parts of the Torah revisit Mount Sinai's depiction and language because this moment teaches that people cannot approach God safely on their own. It also explains the role of God's word in redeeming humanity.

WHO IS IN THE TORAH?

God is the Torah's primary character. The Torah directly describes what God says and does, but it also shows God's good and powerful presence in surprises that overturn expectations. It promises a good ending for God and humanity.

The first man and his wife, Adam and Eve, also play an important role. Their life with God in the beginning typifies and anticipates what happens to others throughout the Torah, especially when God encounters the nation Israel at Mount Sinai. In their stories, the man Adam and the nation Israel are both near God, but they are sent away from Him in exile because of sin. Both also receive a promise from God that they may return to live life with Him in the last days through a promised person, a "seed."

The Torah features several other flawed people, whose lives foreshadow this "seed" who will save humanity:

- Noah walks with God by obeying His instructions and yet also sins like Adam. He is not this promised person, but this promised person's story will echo parts of Noah's story.

- Abram, who is also called Abraham, portrays how a sinful person can still live life with God and learn to trust Him. Abraham is one of the Torah's two great prophets. He fails tremendously in his life, yet God changes his heart while he waits for God's promised person.
- Abraham's nephew, Lot, walks with God for a while but goes away into exile.
- Abraham's promise of a promised person is then carried to the next generation to his son Isaac, as he sends his other son Ishmael away into exile.
- The promise moves next from Isaac to his son Jacob, while his other son Esau goes into exile. Jacob, whose name is also Israel, has twelve sons whose descendants become the nation of Israel. God calls this nation to approach Him at Mount Sinai.

The names of Jacob's twelve sons become the names of Israel's twelve tribes. Three of Jacob's sons prove especially important: Joseph, Judah, and Levi. Joseph is betrayed by his brothers but remains faithful to God. His life resembles the life the promised person will have, but, remarkably, the promised person will come from his brother Judah's family. Levi proves important because the Torah's second major prophet will come from his family: Moses. Moses leads the nation Israel out of Egypt but fails to bring them on Mount Sinai and into the land of Canaan. Someone greater than Moses will need to come.

The Torah repeatedly teaches about this promised person. The Torah knows Him as:

- The seed of the woman;
- The seed of Abraham, Isaac, and Jacob;
- The promised king from the tribe of Judah who looks like Joseph;

- The Prophet like Moses;
- The word the nation Israel asked for at Mount Sinai.

KEY TAKEAWAYS

Every reader of the Torah has something to learn from God's relationship with Israel. The way that God cares for the nation Israel before, during, and after Israel's time at Mount Sinai is the way that He will care for all people. The Torah uses narratives, poems, law codes, and genealogies to show how Adam's and the nation of Israel's failures to live with God teach us about God's presence by His word.

GENESIS 1–11

The Creation of All Things and Man's Sin and Exile

> "So God created man in his own image."
> —Genesis 1:27

The Bible begins with the book of Genesis. Its opening chapters teach how God creates all things, including humanity, and how humankind falls from this good state into our broken world. The sin of the first man and woman spreads across the generations to every man and woman. The author surrounds several genealogies with unexpected accounts of how God answers humankind's sin with both death and life.

GENESIS 1–2: CREATION

"In the beginning God created the heaven and the earth" (Gen 1:1). This opening sentence unveils a contrast between God as Creator and His creation, which the rest of the Bible explains. The creation is not the Creator.

"In the Beginning"

Genesis' first word, *bereshiyt*, translates as "In the beginning." It may also translate as "By wisdom" or "By the firstborn." While "in the beginning" is the best translation, one ancient Jewish commentary reads, "In the beginning, by wisdom, by the firstborn, God created the heavens and the earth."

God's Spirit hovers over the waters, and He speaks ten times to form a land for people to live with God: the garden in Eden. God creates man, Adam, from the dust of the ground and brings him into the garden. It is a promised land where God reveals His goodness. Adam speaks as God's prophet, naming the animals. He serves and guards the garden as His priest. He also rules as God's king, and is commanded to multiply and fill the earth. God provides Adam with food from any of the trees, but He forbids Adam from eating from the tree of the knowledge of good and evil. He will surely die on the day he eats it. God calls Adam to rule the whole creation and then makes His goodness most visible in the forming of his wife, Eve. Upon seeing her, Adam proclaims Eve's value, dignity, humanity, and unity with him. This joining of the first man to the first woman teaches God's good plan to bless all humanity by His word and commands. What God wants is good for all people. It brings His life, value, and purpose to all generations.

GENESIS 3: THE FALL

A serpent approaches Eve to question God's word. Her answer echoes God's words but also adds to them. She rightly understands that God's command to humanity (not to eat the fruit of this tree) applies to her, but she unfortunately adds to God's instruction: They are not to touch this tree at all. This added law proves powerless against the serpent's counsel, her own desires, and her husband's silence. The serpent promises she will not die but will instead have her eyes opened and be like God, knowing good and evil. She eats from the fruit of the tree and gives some to her husband, who is with her. Their eyes open, but an unintended change takes place. Having only known "good," they now know "good and evil."

They hear God's voice and try to hide. His questions teach even as His words probe. God seeks their repentance but instead finds blame-shifting. God's word curses the serpent and pronounces tragedy for humankind. God exiles them from the garden and His presence. He says the "seed" of the serpent will be at odds with the "seed" of the woman, but promises a final victory for the "seed" of the woman. This promise sets Adam's hope on the future arrival of this man, the "seed," who will return His people to God's presence. They and their future descendants will live and die out of the garden in an exile of trouble and toil, a slow death. God guards the way back to the tree of life with a cherubim, an angelic being, who wields a flaming sword.

GENESIS 4–11: SIN'S SPREAD

Humanity's conflicts multiply in exile, but God remains present by His word, even with Adam and Eve's first two sons, Cain and Abel. God approves of a sacrifice Abel makes to Him but rejects his brother Cain's, because his heart was not right. He warns Cain to avoid sin, but Cain rejects God's instruction and murders his brother. God judges Cain and provides a "sign" to keep him alive after Cain's anguish and grief overwhelm him. God also provides a replacement for Abel: Seth.

A genealogy of ten names follows. All ten men die within the genealogy except Enoch and Noah. "Enoch walked with God: and he was not" (Gen 5:24). He does not die but is simply there no more. God took him. Noah also walks with God, but the rest of humanity delights in sin. God judges all people by sending a flood to end the harm of these sins, but He also offers a path for life. Noah obeys God and builds a boat, an ark, that will hold eight people, two of every animal, and seven of every "clean" animal for sacrifices at the end of the pending flood. The flood arrives, and only those with Noah survive. The rest of humankind dies.

As Noah's family eventually exits the boat after the flood subsides, Noah receives a covenant from God, a binding agreement sealed by sacrifice: God will not judge the earth in this same way again. He will not send another global flood, but He will still send a last judgment. Noah's life suggests he might be the promised "seed," but he sins by drinking of the fruit after he steps out of the boat into the "new world" that God lays out before him. He is not the promised person. His son Ham also sins in this moment, leading to the cursing of Ham's son, Canaan. All humanity derives from Noah's flawed family.

Humanity reaches a valley in Babel and does not want to be scattered. They build a tower so that they might make a "name" for themselves. God visits the tower and sees that their unity in having one language will allow them to fulfill their evil desires. He divides their words into many languages and scatters humanity everywhere. Another genealogy of ten names follows. The tenth man is Abram, whose father, Terah, fails to lead his family to the land of Canaan. Abram and his wife, Sarai, with his nephew, Lot, live just outside the land of Canaan.

KEY TAKEAWAYS

Humankind quickly loses the good gift of a land to live with God because of man's sin in God's presence. Sin multiplies through every person in every place. Despite this spreading sin and God's deadly judgment, life also emerges as God's word remains present to guide and lead fallen people, especially Noah. Through his story and eventual failure, we see a growing need for and anticipation of God's promised and future deliverer, the "seed" of the woman. Perhaps this promised person will come through Abram's family.

GENESIS 12–50

God Walks with Abraham's Family

> "And he believed in the LORD; and he counted it to him for righteousness."
> —Genesis 15:6

This section of Genesis highlights Abram, also known as Abraham. His family walks with God through God's promise to provide them a "seed" who will bring humanity to the land where God dwells. This promise passes or moves from one generation to the next as they await its future fulfillment. It passes from Abraham to Isaac to Jacob. At a key moment, God changes Jacob's name to Israel. Despite the family's many failures, God's presence brings them and others life in unexpected ways.

GENESIS 12–25: ABRAHAM AND ISAAC

Abram obeys God, leading his barren wife, Sarai, and nephew, Lot, to Canaan. God promises that this elderly and childless couple's descendants, their "seed," will possess this land. Lot divides from Abram to live near Sodom, a place of overwhelming sexual sin, but he is captured in a great battle. Abram miraculously rescues him.

Despite this victory, Abram fears God will not keep His promise. God assures him that his "seed" will be numerous, and Abram believes Him. Nonetheless, Sarai asks Abram to bear a son through her handmaiden. Ishmael is born from this plan, but God confirms that Abram's promised "seed" will come from Sarai. God changes their names to Abraham and Sarah and commands him to circumcise every male. Abraham immediately obeys. God also destroys Sodom and Gomorrah for its great sexual sin, but He rescues Lot from this destruction because of Abraham's plea for mercy on his behalf.

God finally provides a son for Abraham through Sarah: Isaac. When conflict arises between Sarah and the handmaiden, grieving Abraham sends Ishmael away. God tests Abraham, ordering him to sacrifice Isaac, his only remaining son. On the walk to Mount Moriah to sacrifice the son he loves, Abraham declares he and Isaac will go on the mountain, worship God, and return together because God will provide a sacrificial lamb. As Abraham readies to slaughter Isaac, God commands Abraham to not harm him. God knows that Abraham fears Him. Surprisingly, God provides a sacrificial ram, not a lamb. People will wait for the promised lamb to come on God's mountain.

Why Does God Ask Abraham to Sacrifice Isaac?

God does not want Abraham to kill Isaac; it's a test. He tests Abraham to see if he loves and fears Him. Abraham's time with God changes his heart and yields life with God for him and Isaac on Mount Moriah. Although he expects death in God's presence, his faith and obedience lead to life with God for Abraham and his son.

After Sarah's death, Isaac marries Rebekah, who comforts him in his grief. God gives her twin boys. The older son, Esau, despises his birthright, which entitles him to his father's inheritance, and gives it to his brother, Jacob. He prefers eating stew to his own birthright.

GENESIS 26–36: ISAAC AND JACOB

When he is nearing death, Isaac aims to bless Esau, but Jacob steals his blessing. Jacob flees Esau's wrath and departs Canaan to seek out Rebekah's brother, Laban. On his way, God reveals to Jacob that Canaan is "God's house." Jacob asks God to be with him and return him to Canaan. In his exile from Canaan, Jacob works for Laban seven years to marry his younger daughter, Rachel. At the end of the seven years, Laban deceives Jacob and gives him his older daughter, Leah, instead. To marry Rachel, Jacob works seven more years.

God blesses Jacob in exile by giving him eleven sons through Leah, Rachel, and their two handmaidens. Leah births Reuben, Simeon, Levi, Judah, Issachar, and Zebulun. Handmaidens give him Dan, Naphtali, Gad, and Asher. Finally, his second wife Rachel births Joseph before returning to Canaan.

Jacob arrives in Canaan, fearing his brother's vengeance. The night before Esau arrives, Jacob wrestles with a man. While wrestling, Jacob receives a new name from God: Israel. Astonishingly, when Esau arrives, his wrath is gone. The brothers find peace. Jacob stays in Canaan, but Rachel dies in Bethlehem giving birth to Jacob's twelfth son, Benjamin.

GENESIS 37–50: JOSEPH

Jacob favors Joseph, so Joseph's brothers hate him. Their hatred grows when Joseph dreams that he will rule over them. They plot to murder him but instead sell him to people going to Egypt. The brothers cover Joseph's coat in goat's blood to deceive Jacob, who believes Joseph is dead.

In Egypt, Joseph serves an Egyptian officer. God is with Joseph, blessing the Egyptian's house. This officer's wife lies about Joseph and sends him to prison, but God is with him there too. He blesses the prison because of Joseph. Sometime later, Egypt's king, Pharaoh, sends his cupbearer and baker to this prison, where dreams trouble them. Joseph interprets their dreams, and afterward the cupbearer returns to serve Pharaoh. Joseph lingers in prison until dreams disturb Pharaoh. Joseph explains that Pharaoh's dreams reveal God's plans. God will bring a seven-year famine after seven years of plenty. Pharaoh sets Joseph as ruler. He guides Egypt to store food for seven years. When the famine hits, everyone comes to Joseph for food.

The famine spreads to Canaan, so Jacob orders his sons to buy food in Egypt. He will not send Benjamin, the only remaining son of his beloved, deceased Rachel. The brothers do not recognize Joseph when they arrive, but Joseph recognizes them. He tests them, charging them with being spies. To prove they are not spies, they must bring their youngest brother, Benjamin. Joseph sends them back to Canaan and also tests them by setting the money they used for the purchase in their bags. When they realize the money is there, they believe that they will wrongly and eventually be charged with stealing the money.

The brothers explain to Jacob that they may only return to Egypt with Benjamin. Jacob refuses to send him, but the famine becomes too great. He finally sends Benjamin, preparing his heart to see him die. The brothers expect wrath from Joseph because of the extra money, but the sight of Benjamin warms Joseph's heart.

Joseph gives the brothers a feast and sends them back to Canaan, but he also slips his special cup into Benjamin's sack as a test. The brothers are accused of stealing this cup, which is found in Benjamin's bag. Benjamin must remain enslaved in Egypt, so Judah approaches Joseph and offers to take Benjamin's place since Benjamin's absence will lead to Jacob's death from his own intense grief. Judah's repentance softens Joseph's heart. Joseph reveals himself to his brothers and has them, their families, and their father, Jacob, join them in Egypt to live freely while they wait for God to return them to Canaan. They will be in Egypt for generations.

Joseph's Tests

Joseph tests his brothers by requiring them to bring back Benjamin because he remembered his dreams. This test resembles God's test of Abraham because Joseph asks Jacob to give up his only remaining son from Rachel. Joseph wants his brothers and their father to find life in the famine and after it. God patiently changes Jacob's heart through the test.

KEY TAKEAWAYS

God cares for Abraham's family, among many others. They receive and carry on from one generation to the next the same promise from God. He will provide a "seed" who will bring them to the land where God dwells. Each generation struggles to live in that promise. This large, growing, and flawed family waits in Egypt for this promised person to come.

EXODUS 1–18

God Rescues His Exiled People

> "The LORD shall fight for you."
> —Exodus 14:14

Years after Joseph and his brothers died in Egypt, their descendants become enslaved there. God blesses Jacob's family, the nation Israel, despite afflictions (harsh treatment) from their Egyptian masters. In these trying times, God raises up Moses to be the nation Israel's leader. Through Moses, God also calls on Pharaoh, Egypt's king, to let Israel go and worship God. The king's stubborn resistance multiplies the Egyptians' agony as God makes Himself known to them. In the end, God miraculously delivers Israel through the death of the firstborn and the parting of the Red Sea on their way to Mount Sinai.

EXODUS 1–4: GOD CALLS MOSES TO DELIVER ISRAEL

God blesses the nation Israel in Egypt, but Pharaoh views these people as a threat. This king curses Israel, but each curse becomes a blessing. He afflicts their labor, but the population of Israel still multiplies. He commands two midwives to murder all of Israel's newborn boys, but they fear God and let them live. Pharaoh commands his people to drown these baby boys. One Israelite woman, however, hides her newly born son until forced to set him in a basket on the river's edge. While the baby's older sister, Miriam, watches, Pharaoh's daughter shows the baby compassion. Pharaoh's daughter permits Miriam's mother to nurse the boy. After weaning him, she returns him to Pharaoh's daughter, who names him Moses.

Years later, Moses sees an Egyptian hurting an Israelite, so he murders the man. Believing no one saw his crime, he later confronts two Israelite men who are fighting. After rejecting Moses' call for peace and his leadership, one of them questions whether Moses plans to murder him too. His sin is known, so Moses flees. Then he rescues the daughters of a priest, Jethro, and marries one of them.

Later at Mount Sinai, Moses sees a burning bush. God calls to Moses from it to tell him He will deliver Israel. He commands Moses to lead Israel, but Moses feels unfit. God promises Moses His presence and a sign that God sent him on this mission. This sign is not the burning bush or the many plagues He will perform in Egypt. The sign will be when all of God's people worship Him on His mountain.

God sends Moses to Pharoah so that God Himself (through Moses) may bring Israel out of Egypt to live with Him. Most importantly, God provides Moses His proper name, "I AM THAT I AM" (Exo 3:14). Because Moses fears speaking for God, his brother Aaron will speak to Pharaoh. Together, Aaron and Moses will perform signs before Israel, Pharaoh, and Egypt.

What Does God's Proper Name Mean?

God's proper name is "I AM THAT I AM." It means "I am with you and good to you." It is typically written in the third person "HE IS" with the four Hebrew letters: YHWH. When the English Bible states *LORD* in capital letters, that name references God's proper name.

EXODUS 5:1–15:21:
GOD APPROACHES EGYPT

Moses commands Pharaoh to send away God's people, the nation Israel, so that they may worship Him. Pharaoh refuses and instead hardens the labor of the people of Israel, so they cry out against Moses and what he has said for God. God promises to rescue Israel through signs—in this case, plagues—so that the Egyptians will know God. Through Moses, God will approach Pharaoh with ten plagues so that Egypt may live with God in the end. He is seeking to save the Egyptians by demonstrating who He is.

The Ten Plagues

God then sends the plagues: He turns the Nile River to blood, brings frogs all over Egypt, and transforms Egypt's dust into gnats. God follows these with swarms of flies, and afflicts Egypt's livestock in the field with a plague. Pharaoh refuses to heed God's word, and hardens his heart with each new plague. God then sends boils on Egypt and their animals, but now God hardens Pharaoh's heart so that His miraculous wonders may multiply and the Egyptians may come to know Him.

After God brings hail against Egypt, Pharaoh confesses his sin. When the hail ends, Pharaoh hardens his heart again. God promises to send locusts against Pharaoh and Egypt, so Pharaoh agrees to let Israel go if only the men will depart. God and Moses do not bargain, so the locusts cover Egypt. God hardens Pharaoh's heart once again. Then God brings a blinding darkness over Egypt. Pharaoh agrees that all Israel may go, but they may not take their animals. God and Moses still do not bargain, so God again hardens Pharaoh's heart.

Understanding Why God Hardens Pharaoh's Heart

God acts through people without approving of them and for different purposes than they plan. Pharaoh hardens his heart against God because Pharaoh views himself as sovereign over all things. He is wrong and learning a painful lesson in the process. God hardens Pharaoh's heart so that God's name will be known and people will trust Him.

The Passover is the last sign, the tenth plague. In it, God will put to death every firstborn male. If a family sets the blood of a sacrificed lamb on its door, the firstborn will live. God does indeed put firstborns to death all over Egypt. There is life, however, in houses with lamb blood on the door. Finally, the grieving Pharaoh, who has lost his firstborn, relents, and God's people leave. By a pillar of cloud and fire, God leads them to the Red Sea.

The Parting of the Red Sea

God hardens Pharaoh's heart one more time, however. Pharaoh sees the nation Israel seemingly trapped by the Red Sea. His army pursues them. When the terrified Israelites see the army approaching, they fear that God intends to kill them. Moses answers their fear by saying, "The LORD shall fight for you" (Exo 14:14). He stretches out his hand and divides the waters. Israel walks across on dry land while the pillar of fire holds Egypt back.

After Israel makes it through, the Egyptians pursue. God hardens their chariot wheels, as He had done to their hearts. Facing death, some Egyptians cry out to flee because they have learned what Israel is to learn: God fights for Israel. Moses raises his hands, and a wall of water kills the Egyptians. In the aftermath, Israel celebrates this victory as a preview of Canaan's future conquest and the future fulfillment of God's promise to Abraham.

EXODUS 15:22–18:27: GOD LEADS ISRAEL TOWARD MOUNT SINAI

God leads the nation Israel through the wilderness by a pillar of cloud and fire. Facing hunger and thirst, Israel complains about God, but He sustains them with food and water in the wilderness. God provides them a special bread from heaven, called *manna*, and water from a rock. Nonetheless, weary Israel complains. The Amalekites, a part of Esau's family, attack Israel, but God gives Israel victory. God also promises to wipe out Amalek at the end of time. Jethro, Moses' father-in-law, hears the good news of God delivering Israel and worships God. As God's priest, Jethro leads Moses and Israel's elders to worship Him. Jethro then offers God's counsel to Moses.

KEY TAKEAWAYS

In this action-packed section, God blesses exiled Israel. Even when a powerful king curses Israel, God sustains and blesses His people. After hearing their cries, God raises up a deliverer: Moses. He leads them out of Egypt with great signs and plagues so that the Egyptians may know who God is. God takes care of Israel as they travel through the wilderness so that they may worship God on His mountain, Mount Sinai.

EXODUS 19–40

God Descends on Mount Sinai and Provides His Word

"And ye shall be unto me a kingdom of priests."
—Exodus 19:6

Israel arrives at Mount Sinai in hope that *all* people will go up on the mountain to be with God. When they do not go up, their disobedience unveils God's patient mercy with them. He provides them His word and a covenant with many laws that will keep them close to God and God's tent, the tabernacle. Even after they worship an idol of God rather than God Himself, God again shows them mercy. He leads them to build the tabernacle with God's partial presence.

EXODUS 19–24: GOD DESCENDS ON MOUNT SINAI

Israel encamps before Mount Sinai, where God wants them to obey His voice like Abraham did at Mount Moriah. He tells them to keep God's covenant so that they may become God's kingdom of priests and His holy nation. He warns Moses to sanctify, which means to set apart as holy, Israel, "for [on] the third day the LORD will come down in the sight of all the people upon mount Sinai" (Exo 19:11). Under penalty of death, Israel must stay back from the mountain until the trumpet blasts, at which time they will go up on the mountain. On the third day, they see and hear God's presence on the mountain.

When the trumpet blasts, however, they tremble and do not go up, disobeying God.

The People Disobey

Being faced with the call to go on the mountain, Israel instead fears dying in God's presence, trembles at the sight of God's Kingdom, and disobeys Him. After Israel's failure to ascend the mountain, God now warns them *not* to go on Mount Sinai. They must stay back. God answers their disobedience by giving Israel a covenant of laws that begins with Ten Commandments. These core laws teach how to live safely near God.

After detailing these initial laws, the author flashes back to the moment of God descending on the mountain. Israel's leaders ask Moses to draw near to God and hear God's word for them. If they continue to hear God's word directly, they will die. They ask for God's word to come through Moses because they desire to be close to God. God's words coming through Moses' words make life with God possible. He moves Israel from a bad fear of death in His presence, which pulls Israel away from Him, to a good fear of God, which draws Israel close to Him.

Applying the Ten Commandments

Moses provides Israel with additional laws that clarify how Israel should apply the Ten Commandments. One commandment warns that anyone who worships another god, an idol, "shall be utterly destroyed" (Exo 22:20). This complete destruction of idols is also known as being placed under the ban. Those who worship idols will die in God's presence under the ban.

In addition, God promises that His Messenger with God's name in Him, who will be God Himself in His complete presence, will eliminate Canaan's idols, complete Canaan's conquest, and fulfill

Abraham's promise that a seed will come to bring them to the land where God dwells. Israel agrees to this Mosaic Covenant of laws. Afterward, Moses goes alone on the mountain for forty days.

EXODUS 25–31: GOD EXPLAINS THE TABERNACLE'S DESIGN

God instructs Moses to make the tabernacle according to the pattern He shows him on the mountain. This tabernacle is a preview of heaven on earth—a tent where Israel can approach God and yet live through repeated sacrifices. The tent itself will contain the Most Holy Place, where God will set the Ark of the Covenant. Above this Ark will be two statues of cherubim, winged angels. God's mercy seat and partial presence will be there and will preview His complete presence. From this mercy seat, God will give Moses His commands.

EXODUS 32–34: THE GOLDEN CALF

The people gather against Moses' brother, Aaron, and demand an idol, or image, of God. Aaron makes a golden calf that Israel worships as their God. They should be destroyed under the ban because of such idolatry, but Moses pleads for mercy. Because the laws were disobeyed, when Moses comes down the mountain, he shatters the Ten Commandments, destroys the golden calf, and rallies the tribe of Levi to slaughter three thousand Israelites caught in this sin. The sin stops, but the nation Israel needs God's mercy.

Moses offers to be annihilated for Israel's sake, but God must judge *all* sin and wipe out of His book everyone who sins. He directs Moses to lead Israel to Canaan, but God's complete presence will not go with them. If God were now to send His complete presence with them, He would destroy Israel and their idols before they reached Canaan rather than the idols in Canaan. Instead, God will send lesser messengers before them to keep them alive until the last days. Their judgment is delayed, not removed. God's complete presence will assuredly punish Israel for its sin, but for now, God's mercy requires lesser messengers.

Who Is God's Messenger?

Exodus 23:20–26 promises that God will send His Messenger with His name in Him, His complete presence, to carry Israel to Canaan and end its idolatry. After the golden calf, God sends lesser messengers so that God's complete presence will not destroy Israel on the way to Canaan.

God promises that His partial presence will accompany Moses but not His complete presence. Moses wants to see God's glory, but no person may live after seeing God's full glory and complete presence. When God shows Moses part of His glory, He declares His goodness in both justice and mercy. God offers life to those who seek Him and yet also punishes all sin.

Moses then sets the Ten Commandments on new stones, and God answers Israel's sin by adding new laws that reapply the Ten Commandments.

EXODUS 35–40: ISRAEL BUILDS THE TABERNACLE

After God's mercy at the golden calf that kept Israel alive near Him, He calls Israel to contribute to the tabernacle's construction. An overwhelming group of Israelites give the items needed to build it. God's Spirit equips two men to lead in building the tabernacle's parts according to the exact pattern God showed Moses on the mountain. After Moses inspects their work, God's glory fills the tabernacle.

KEY TAKEAWAYS

God's Kingdom descends on top of Mount Sinai. His mercy appears when Israel does not go up on the mountain as directed. God leads Israel from a bad fear of God to a good fear that seeks to be near Him by His word. God's mercy shows up again after Israel worships the golden calf. He delays their judgment and allows His partial presence in the tabernacle.

LEVITICUS

Approaching God at the Tabernacle

> "Be holy: for I the LORD your God am holy."
> —Leviticus 19:2

Israel needs sacrifices to approach God at the tabernacle. As such, Leviticus describes many different types of sacrifices, which partially and temporarily atone for, or fix, sins. The book's laws also teach the ritual cleanliness and holiness needed to be near God, and the laws address those both in the context of larger principles and specific situations. In addition, these laws periodically echo moments and sins of Genesis' narratives. These laws and their appointed times of worship intersect with continuous narratives to show Israel needs God's laws.

LEVITICUS 1–10: LAWS FOR SACRIFICES

God commands Israel to offer sacrifices for various reasons. For example, they can bring burnt offerings, grain offerings, peace offerings, sin offerings, and guilt offerings so that they may approach God in the tabernacle.

These sacrifices of animals, grain, flour, drinks, oil, incense, and even personal vows will teach about sin's great cost. They will delay God's wrath on the person and the people in the same way that the ram sacrificed for Isaac on Mount Moriah delayed Isaac's death. In this way, these sacrifices partially atone for the sin of the repentant Israelite.

With a series of his own sacrifices, Moses initiates Aaron's and his sons' priesthood. Only Aaron and his sons may serve as priests in the tabernacle. The tribe of Levi, Aaron's and Moses' tribe, takes care of the tabernacle wherever Israel goes. Having been prepared by his brother, Aaron begins his priestly work with his own sacrificial acts. After Moses and Aaron depart the tabernacle, God's glory appears and consumes Aaron's sacrifices. The new priesthood begins well.

Unfortunately, two of Aaron's sons, Nadab and Abihu, offer unauthorized fire before God. Fire comes out from God and devours them. While not detailing which aspect of the laws they broke, Moses teaches a larger lesson. People must treat God as holy when they approach Him. Moses fears more death among the brand-new priesthood, so he orders Aaron to eat the required sacrifice. When Moses returns, shockingly, Aaron burns up the sacrifice without eating it. Moses fears Aaron's death. Aaron, however, rightly teaches that God will not accept him eating the sacrifice on the day his sons die. His grieving heart is not right. The heart's condition matters greatly to God in sacrifices. Priests must teach and practice God's wisdom, as Aaron does here.

LEVITICUS 11–15: LAWS OF CLEANLINESS

After the fire devours Aaron's sons, and after Aaron and Moses debate whether to eat the sacrifice, Moses provides laws from God about what an Israelite should eat. These laws define certain animals as unclean for Israel. They should not be eaten by anyone in the nation of Israel. These food laws are the first part of the cleanliness laws.

Marking something or someone as "unclean" declares it unfit for drawing close to God at the tabernacle. If someone sins, they are unclean. However, uncleanness can result from the impact of others' sins, even Adam's first sin. A person can be unclean while obeying God, or as part of a tragic situation without fault. An unclean person is unsafe near the tabernacle because his presence may result in his own death or the deaths of others.

These laws also specify how an Israelite may be declared clean. After detailing what is clean and unclean to eat, Moses defines a woman as unclean after giving birth because of the blood, echoing Eve's story in Genesis and her birth pains. The woman giving birth walks in the consequences of Eve's sin and passes on such consequences to her daughter. Those with skin diseases, bodily discharges, and houses with mildew are also unsafe near the tabernacle.

Uncleanness in Male versus Female Births

Because a mother passes on Eve's pain in birth to a daughter but not to a son, she is unclean longer when she gives birth to a girl as compared to giving birth to a boy. This law underscores the continuing effects of the first sin.

LEVITICUS 16: THE DAY OF ATONEMENT

The tabernacle's design sets God's presence in the Most Holy Place. Once a year on the Day of Atonement, the High Priest enters the Most Holy Place. The High Priest has safe access to God's presence for one day a year through making several sacrifices for himself and goats for the people of Israel. One goat is sacrificed, but the other is the scapegoat. The priests lay their hands upon this scapegoat, setting all of Israel's sins on the animal. Afterward, they send the animal and Israel's sins away. There is no atoning for Israel's sins without this annual day.

LEVITICUS 17–27: THE HOLINESS LAWS

God commands holiness from the nation Israel in the final half of Leviticus. They must reflect God's character and practice God's commands because He is their God. Israel must not follow foreign sexual practices. These prohibitions also rebuke the sexual acts of Israel's ancestors as read in Genesis. God rejects, for example, homosexuality and having multiple wives among other sexual sins because marriage and sex should pass on God's life to the next generation. Sexual sins yield tragic consequences and bring God's judgment. As such, these holiness laws challenge the priests to guard their own lives and bodies.

If Israel obeys these laws, they find blessing. If they disobey these laws, curses follow. Both blessings and curses teach Israel that God Himself is their greatest blessing. If they live with God by obeying, they will find good. If they forget God, on the other hand, God allows them to discover idolatry's consequences via curses that seek Israel's eventual return to God. As He details the implications of Israel's response to His laws, the curses outnumber and overwhelm the blessings. Exile from God is the greatest curse. Yet, in exile, Israel may confess its sins and return to God because God will remember His covenant with Abraham: A seed will bring them to the land where God dwells.

KEY TAKEAWAYS

Leviticus details how Israel can stay close to God. God's holiness demands Israel's holiness, yet He also provides a way to atone for their sin and lack of holiness so as to lengthen their time with God. The sacrifices and appointed times of worship will delay God's wrath. Obeying God brings genuine blessings, including more time with God Himself, while disobeying God yields curses, including exile, so that Israel may repent and find real life with God in the end because of God's promise to Abraham.

NUMBERS

In the Wilderness

"I shall see him, but not now: I shall behold him, but not nigh: there shall come
a Star out of Jacob, and a Sceptre shall rise out of Israel."
—Num 24:17

Israel departs for the land of Canaan but never gets there. The journey
from Sinai echoes the journey to Sinai. After departing the mountain, the
people repeat the same sins from before they received the law codes. The
nation of Israel again complains, and other nations fight against them.
Israel fails to go up into the land of Canaan because they fear death, as
they did at Mount Sinai. Except for two persons, God judges this first generation by having them wander and die in the wilderness. He brings the
second generation to the edge of the promised land with hope.

NUMBERS 1–10: MOUNT SINAI

At Mount Sinai, God commands a census of Israel's fighting men
from the twelve tribes. Aaron's tribe of Levi is not counted because
they have no set part of the land as their inheritance. God is their
inheritance. Aaron's sons serve as priests, making sacrifices at the
tabernacle. The other Levites take care of the tabernacle itself and
the objects inside it. After a Passover feast, which celebrates how
God delivered Israel out of Egypt by passing over the death of the
firstborn sons and with two silver trumpets blaring, Israel departs
for Canaan, being led by God's pillar of cloud and fire.

The Tribes of Israel

Israel's twelve tribes come from Jacob's sons: Reuben, Simeon, Levi, Judah, Dan, Naphtali, Gad, Asher, Issachar, Zebulun, Joseph, and Benjamin. Joseph's oldest two sons, Ephraim and Manasseh, are also declared tribes, and Levi is usually left out, since God is their inheritance, not land.

NUMBERS 11–21: THE WILDERNESS

Israel again grumbles. They desire meat, not God's manna. God pours out His Spirit on seventy elders who for one moment prophesy and speak for God, helping Moses lead the people. Moses desires all God's people to have His Spirit on them, but that time is not yet. God then provides the people with an abundance of quail for meat. Some follow their desires for meat rather than God, and they die from a plague as they eat the quail. Then, Aaron and Miriam critique Moses, but God rebukes them.

Israel reaches the edge of the land of Canaan and sends twelve spies to scout out the land for forty days. Ten spies report that the land is good but filled with cities too strong and fortified to overcome. The spies Caleb and Joshua, however, encourage Israel to go into the land. Fearing death, Israel complains, plans to return to Egypt, and desires a new leader. God judges them, but Moses asks God to show them mercy. God sends Israel to wander in the wilderness for forty years. All the adults of that generation, except Joshua and Caleb, will die there.

A Levite named Korah leads many Israelites to rebel against Moses and Aaron, but on the next day, God splits the ground and it swallows the rebels. The angered Israelites want Moses to die. Nonetheless, Moses through Aaron intercedes for them. After Miriam dies, Israel finds itself again without water. God commands Moses to gather the congregation and speak to the rock so that He can bring out water. Moses rightly takes his staff and assembles the people, but he speaks to them, not the rock, striking it twice. Despite the tensions between what God commands and what Moses does, water comes out of the rock.

Even with the water flow, God rebukes Moses and Aaron. They do not have the faith to lead Israel because they did not sanctify God before the people. Israel will need someone with greater faith to lead them. Shortly thereafter, Aaron dies, and his son Eleazar becomes the High Priest.

Israel suffers conflict with many nations in the wilderness. Israel fights Canaanite and Amorite kings who war against them, with Israel winning victories over the land east of Canaan. Israel also encounters nations from Abraham's family: Edom and Moab. These nations oppose Israel's journey through their lands, but God lets them pass through without conquering them.

NUMBERS 22–25: BALAAM

The Moabite king Balak sees Israel as a threat and calls a non-Israelite prophet named Balaam to curse them. Balaam agrees to curse Israel, which God allows after restricting the prophet's words to blessing Israel. Balaam declares the fates of Israel and the nations in the last days: As God brought Israel out of Egypt, so Balaam promises God will bring His King, the "seed" of Abraham, out of Egypt in the last days.

NUMBERS 26–36: THE WILDERNESS AND LAND DISTRIBUTION

Moses counts the people of Israel a second time. Despite all the sin and death since they left Mount Sinai, there are still about the same number of people in Israel. The laws do not fix Israel's problems, but God sustains His people through them.

The law codes have limits and are not designed to anticipate every situation, as the book shows when a man with no sons and five daughters dies. This man, Zelophehad, cannot pass the land inheritance to his daughters. The deceased man's name will perish in the land if this is the case, so Moses adds a law for his daughters to receive his land.

In these journeys throughout the wilderness, God chooses Joshua to succeed Moses. The tribes of Reuben and Gad ask Moses to give them the already conquered land east of Canaan. Moses fears they are repeating their parents' refusal to go into Canaan, but they pledge to fight in Canaan for their brothers. He agrees to let Reuben, Gad, and half of Manasseh's tribe inherit land beyond Canaan. Moses also sets aside forty-eight cities for the Levites. They will live among the other tribes because no one part of the land is theirs.

Numbers ends with Moses adding yet another law: Zelophehad's five daughters must marry men from their own tribe in order to keep their land.

KEY TAKEAWAYS

When Israel refuses to go into the land of Canaan, God judges that generation by having them die in the wilderness in a forty-year wandering. By the end of Numbers, the first generation is dead, and the second generation sits on the edge of the promised land.

DEUTERONOMY

Moses' Words As God's Words

"Moses commanded us a law, even the inheritance of the congregation of Jacob."
—Deuteronomy 33:4

On his last day, Moses interprets God's word in three great speeches. The beginning of Deuteronomy, Deu 1–4, describes the Torah as a story of what happened and will happen after the giving of the law codes. In the book's middle section, Deu 5–26 defines the Torah as law and establishes God's affection for Israel with new laws for a new generation. The final speeches in Deu 29–30 establish Torah as a book and show what God's word will produce. Moses ends his book with poems in Deu 32–33 and then dies. Afterward, we wait for a Prophet Like Moses (the Messiah) to come to do what Moses could not do.

DEUTERONOMY 1–4: TORAH AS STORY

Moses explains the Torah as the story of what happened after the laws were given. He reminds Israel of God's call to depart Sinai, his own failure to lead Israel into Canaan, and God's sustaining presence in forty years of wandering in the wilderness.

Moses also reminds them of the day God descended on Mount Sinai, the day of the assembly. On that day, God spoke from the midst of the fire with Israel, who reached only the base of the mountain. Turning to their future, Moses then promises Israel will go into the land of Canaan under Joshua, but the nation will quickly fall into idolatry. God will scatter Israel among the nations, but from their exile they will seek God completely in the last days. Israel will then finally return to God.

DEUTERONOMY 5–26: TORAH AS LAW

Moses begins his second speech again, describing what occurred at Mount Sinai on the day of the assembly. Moses stood between God and Israel that day because they were afraid of the fire and did not go up on the mountain. Israel's fear of death in God's presence—the bad fear of God—pulled them away from Him.

Moses repeats the Ten Commandments and then revisits the rest of that day, explaining Israel's *good* fear of God. Specifically, Moses reminds Israel how they learned on the day of the assembly that God can speak with man and still live. They asked Moses to hear God so that Moses could tell the people everything God spoke for them. God then called their desire for His word "good." He longed for them to always fear Him and have such a heart to keep His word so that He could always do good to them. A person moved by a good fear of God also loves God at the same time because he draws himself close to God by obeying His word.

The Importance of Mount Sinai in Deuteronomy

From Exodus 19–Numbers 10, the author shows Israel stalling at Mount Sinai because the lesson of their time at the mountain encountering God applies to everyone. Everyone will eventually encounter God in life or in death. At Mount Sinai, we see God and man coming together and learn how man's death in God's presence leads Israel to ask for God's word.

The nation of Israel's future hope stems from this mercy and God's promise to Abraham. On the day of the assembly and forty days later at the golden calf, God's wrath stirred. He readied to wipe out Israel after the golden calf, but God showed mercy.

Moses adds many law codes for Israel, ordering them to destroy the land's idols. He anticipates Israel having a human king who will need to make a copy of the Torah so that he fears God. God also promises that the Prophet Like Moses will come because of what Israel asked for on the day of the assembly. They feared death in God's presence and asked for a word from God through Moses. The Torah derives from that request, but God also asserts that the Prophet Like Moses will come because of their appeal. This Prophet Like Moses will be a word from God who will solve that day's problem: man's death in God's presence.

DEUTERONOMY 27–34: TORAH AS BOOK

When Israel enters Canaan, they will write the Torah on stones and proclaim its blessings and curses. The covenant's curses will overwhelm its blessings. God will eventually bring a faraway nation to fight against disobedient Israel and besiege and scatter them among the nations.

Moses' third speech in Deuteronomy 29–30 clarifies how Israel should respond to these laws by understanding the Torah as God's book. Israel lacks a heart to understand and love God rightly. Any Israelite who falls into idolatry will walk away from God's forgiveness and have his name wiped out. Because of such idolatry, future generations will see the land judged. The nations will ask why God treated the land of Canaan and Israel like Sodom, utterly destroying it. The nations will have the Torah in hand and know that Israel's exile was because they broke the Mosaic Covenant.

From that exile, Israel will return to God because God will change their hearts to love Him completely. God's command to love Him is not impossible because they will have God's word in the Torah. The way God was with Israel at Mount Sinai and the Red Sea is how He will be present with them in the Torah. They will already have God's word near them, calling them to live life with God by trusting His promise to Abraham: a seed is coming to bring them to the land where God dwells.

After challenging Joshua to lead well, Moses warns Israel that they will become more corrupt after he dies. They will provoke God with idolatry, and great calamity will meet them in the last days. God will be Israel's steadfast rock to bless them, but they will sin like all the nations and find themselves in exile among them. This scattering of Israel, however, will bring God's word to the nations. Moses then promises that God's kingdom will cover all mountains as it was at Mount Sinai. Israel and all the nations will live with God forever as His priests.

God leads Moses to the top of Mount Nebo and shows him Canaan. After Moses dies, He buries him. Joshua, being full of the Spirit of wisdom, now leads Israel. The Torah ends with a longing for the Prophet Like Moses, whose work will resemble what Moses did in Egypt.

KEY TAKEAWAYS

Moses affirms God's instruction as a story, a law, and a book. Israel's hope is tied to the last days, when the one promised to Abraham, also called the Prophet Like Moses, will come to change people's hearts so they love God. Moses dies outside the land of Canaan, and the book ends with the reader waiting for God's promises to be fulfilled.

THE PROPHETS, AN OVERVIEW

Israel's Life in the Land of Canaan, Waiting for the Son of David

> "He shall build an house for my name,
> and I will stablish the throne of his kingdom for ever."
> —2 Samuel 7:13

This section gives a brief overview of the second part of the Old Testament, the Prophets. The first half of the Prophets is called the Former Prophets, and it narrates Israel's time in the land of Canaan. The second half of the Prophets is the Latter Prophets, which is primarily a poetic reflection on the Torah that explains what went wrong during Israel's time in the land and what future judgment and hope await Israel and the nations in the last days. The Latter Prophets includes three long books, major prophets, and the Book of the Twelve, which features twelve minor prophets.

THE PROPHETS AS A BOOK

Unlike the English order of the Old Testament, the Hebrew orders pivot from the Torah to the Prophets. The Prophets covers most of the Old Testament and is made up of many smaller books that teach how to read the Torah. The most important chapter of the Prophets is 2 Samuel 7 because it teaches how the person promised to Adam and Eve and to Abraham, Isaac, and Jacob will also be the Son of David.

The Former Prophets begins after Moses' death, with Israel standing outside the land, waiting for God's presence to bring them into the promised land of Canaan. The story ends with Israel exiled from this promised land because they forgot God and delighted in and worshipped idols rather than God. The Former Prophets covers hundreds of years, and the failures of David's descendants teach the reader that the hoped-for Son of David has not yet come.

The Latter Prophets offers a poetic and prophetic explanation of the Former Prophets. This book examines the nation of Israel's constant failures in the promised land and finds hope in God's future work in the last days, as promised to David in 2 Sam 7 and in the Torah's pages.

The narratives of the Former Prophets and the prophetic poetry of the Latter Prophets complement each other. These texts wrestle with the question: Why did God exile His people? God is not abandoning Israel—He depicts their flawed kingdoms as previews of a future and greater King and Kingdom.

THE FORMER PROPHETS

God displays His kingship through the nation of Israel's various leaders. Joshua rules as prophet, priest, and king, and then judges rule after he dies. Saul, David, and Solomon rule as kings over all of Israel. Afterward, many houses and kings rule the rebellious northern kingdom, and David's descendants rule the kingdom of Judah from Jerusalem.

In Joshua's book, Joshua leads Israel into Canaan because God promises to be with Joshua as He was with Moses. In Judges, Israel's situation goes from bad to worse, with an increase in sin, idolatry, and depravity as God uses judges to lead Israel. In 1 and 2 Samuel, the last judge, Samuel, leads God's people as a prophet and priest. He appoints the first king over God's people, Saul, who fails. Then Samuel appoints Israel's second king, David. He desires to build God a house as a permanent version of the tabernacle, but God will not allow that. Instead, God promises the Son of David will build His everlasting house.

Where Did the Book of Ruth Go?

In the three-part order, Ruth is found in the Writings. In *Bible 101*, Ruth follows Proverbs, presenting her as a wise woman. This positioning also helps the reader see how Judges flows directly into 1 Samuel as the same story (Ruth comes between Judges and 1 Samuel in the English version).

In 1 and 2 Kings, David's son Solomon builds a house for God, a temple, but he sins greatly. As a result, God takes half of the kingdom away from Solomon's son when the northern tribes form a new nation. David's and Solomon's descendants rule the southern kingdom, Judah. After exiling the rebellious northern kingdom, God judges the southern kingdom of Judah by raising up, or calling, the nation of Babylon to destroy the temple, Judah, and Jerusalem. The author looks beyond the exiles of the northern and southern kingdoms to find a future hope in the Son of David, who has yet to appear.

THE LATTER PROPHETS

Except for the ending of the Latter Prophets, these prophets lived during the time of 2 Kings. By focusing on the promised Son of David from 2 Sam 7 and the future promises of the Torah, these books depict Israel's failures as a tragedy that leads to their exile from the land. Israel's exile is not the end of God's story with them, however. These Latter Prophets promise a good ending for God and His people. Isaiah and Jeremiah both explain passages from Deuteronomy, critiquing man's sin and offering genuine future hope in it.

The prophet Isaiah's book promises that the Son of David will come to suffer, die, and give his life as a sacrifice that turns God's wrath away from His people so that they may return to Him from exile. Jeremiah sees God coming to judge Judah and Jerusalem so that they may return to Him in the end. Ezekiel reveals God's glory departing Israel, but the book ends with an image of God dwelling with His people in a new Jerusalem with a new temple.

The next twelve books are one book: the Book of the Twelve. They should be read together. The last three books of the Twelve describe the times after Judah's exile. These books show God's people returning to the land of Canaan as promised, but the people discover that they need to wait for the genuine return to God in the last days. The last book, Malachi, warns that God's kingdom is coming, and the readers need to remember the Torah while they wait for that day.

KEY TAKEAWAYS

The Prophets begins with hope for Israel's entry into Canaan, but their continuing idolatry leads to their exile. Despite this failure, God promises the Son of David in 2 Samuel 7, which echoes the Torah's promises of God's coming King. His prophets rebuke sin and encourage the weakened people about God's coming kingdom. The Former Prophets show Israel succumbing to idols despite the promise of the Son of David, and the Latter Prophets frame Israel's tragic exile as part of preparing His people for the coming of His King and Kingdom in the end of the last days: the day of the LORD.

JOSHUA

Israel Fails to Remove Idols from the Land of Canaan

"This book of the law shall not depart out of thy mouth."
—Joshua 1:8

God promises to be with Joshua and Israel through meditating on the Torah. With a miraculous parting of the Jordan River, Joshua leads the people of Israel across it and begins the conquest of Canaan at Jericho. Following God's command to remove the land's idols, Joshua and Israel place Canaan under the ban, devoting Canaan and its idols to total destruction. Surprisingly, some Canaanites become a part of God's people, and some Israelites are placed under the ban for their idolatry. Israel then divides the land among the twelve tribes. By the end of Joshua's life, much of Canaan has been conquered, but not all of it, because Israel struggles to remove idols from their hearts.

JOSHUA 1–4: GOD'S PRESENCE LEADS ISRAEL INTO CANAAN

After Moses' death, God speaks to Joshua, the new leader of Israel. God instructs Joshua to lead Israel across the river and into Canaan to conquer it. He challenges Joshua and Israel to not fear the Canaanites. As God was with Moses, He will be present with Joshua and Israel through the Torah.

Joshua sends two spies to the walled city of Jericho. These spies lay down at the house of a prostitute named Rahab, who hides them from the threat of her king. Rahab asks the spies for mercy when Israel destroys the city because she fears God and seeks life with Him. They agree to save her and all in her house when the city will be destroyed if Rahab will place a scarlet cord in her window and stay in her house. Joshua commands the priests who carry the Ark of the Covenant to step into the river, and the people follow behind them. The water stops flowing and heaps up as the priests step into it, reminding the reader of what God did at the Red Sea. Joshua leads Israel through the river on the dry land. Israel now lives in Canaan.

JOSHUA 5–12: GOD'S PRESENCE CONQUERS MUCH OF THE LAND

Joshua circumcises Israel's men and then approaches Jericho by himself, seeing the commander of God's army, an angel. The angel unexpectedly explains that God is not for Israel or for Israel's adversaries in the upcoming battle. God is for God. He commands Joshua to march Israel's army around Jericho once a day for six days. On the seventh day, they will march around the city seven times and then the people of Israel will shout. The city's walls will collapse. Israel will place Jericho under the ban, slaughtering every man, woman, and child. The people of Israel heed Joshua. When they shout on the seventh day, Jericho's walls collapse. Israel destroys everyone except those with Rahab. Jericho is conquered.

Why Does God Devote the Canaanites to Destruction?

God sets the Canaanites under the ban, devoted to complete destruction, because they worship idols as Israel's conquest brings God's presence to them. God had warned Israel at Mount Sinai of death if they worshipped an idol before Him. Now the same judgment awaits the Canaanites for their idolatry.

Israel must conquer Ai next, but suffers an embarrassing defeat. God will not allow Israel to conquer Ai because of a sinner within Israel named Achan who stole and hid some of the objects marked for God under the ban. The man eventually confesses. Israel executes Achan and his family, removing the sin. Afterward, God allows Joshua and Israel to defeat Ai. Then Joshua makes an altar for sacrifices, copies the Torah onto the land's stones, and leads Israel to pronounce God's blessings and curses.

The Canaanite nation, Gibeon, pretends to be from a faraway land so that Israel will not destroy them. The Gibeonites deceive Joshua and Israel successfully and enter into a peace treaty. Their lie is discovered when Joshua and Israel find the Gibeonites living in Canaan. Israel, however, will keep its promise of peace. Gibeon becomes a part of Israel. When the other Canaanite nations surround Gibeon to destroy it, Joshua saves Gibeon in battle and leads Israel to conquer thirty-one Canaanite kings.

JOSHUA 13–22: GOD'S PRESENCE DIVIDES CANAAN

While Joshua's conquest is great and miraculous, it is incomplete. The aging Joshua allots the land to the twelve tribes of Israel. Each tribe will have a portion of the land except the Levites, who will have God as their inheritance. Reuben, Gad, and half of Manasseh still have land east of Canaan. Within Canaan, the other tribes claim much of their allotted lands, but they fail to drive out the Canaanites completely.

Joshua also establishes cities of refuge where a person who unintentionally kills another without malice or forethought may escape wrath. In addition, he grants Levi forty-eight cities within the lands of the other tribes. They live among the other tribes with no area named after their tribe. With Joshua's role in the conquest ending, he sends home Reuben, Gad, and half of Manasseh to their lands east of Canaan. When news comes that these eastern tribes have erected an altar on the far side of the Jordan, Israel readies to place them under the ban, to devote them to destruction because of idolatry. However, the eastern tribes explain that the altar is not for the worship of idols or the wrong worship of God. It is a memorial altar to remind future Israelites who live in Canaan that the eastern tribes are still family and a part of God's people. This explanation pleases the rest of Israel, and they avoid civil war.

JOSHUA 23–24: GOD'S PRESENCE TEACHES ISRAEL

Joshua offers two speeches to Israel at the end of his life. He reminds them of God's promise to Abraham that brought them to Canaan and His constant provision, challenges them to destroy their idols, and talks of God's good presence with Israel from Abraham to this day. Joshua commits himself and his house to follow God rather than idols, and he calls the people of Israel to do the same. He warns them, however, that they will fail to worship God and will embrace idols. Israel insists they will be faithful. Joshua warns them that they are now witnesses against themselves. They need to get rid of their current idols. Throughout the whole book of Joshua, Israel has been struggling with idols. Afterward, Joshua dies and is buried as God's servant.

God Shows Mercy Despite Israel's Idolatry

God shows mercy on the idolatry of Israel for the sake of God's name being known among all nations so that they, too, may live with Him. Like all nations, Israel struggles with idols. God is patient with Israel because He desires all peoples to find life with Him. All the nations should read the Torah and the Prophets and see how God lived life with Israel because all the nations will follow this same pattern.

KEY TAKEAWAYS

Israel begins its time in Canaan under Joshua, and God is with Joshua as He was with Moses. Obeying God's command to remove idols, Israel sets the Canaanites under the ban. Starting with Jericho, Israel conquers much of the land, but they struggle with their own idols. Some Canaanites, surprisingly, fear God and become a part of Israel. Joshua then divides Canaan and then sends the eastern tribes back to their lands. At the end of Joshua's life, the land is partially conquered. He warns Israel to put away their idols.

JUDGES

Israel Becomes Worse Than Sodom and Gomorrah

> "I will not rule over you, neither shall my son rule over you:
> the LORD shall rule over you."
> —Judges 8:23

The death of Joshua necessitates new leaders over God's people, but these leaders prove flawed. God's Spirit raises up judges, or tribal chieftains, to temporarily deliver, or rescue, Israel. They are not valiant or virtuous. God saves Israel despite these judges, not because of them. With each deliverance, the people of Israel and their leaders fall deeper into sin: a downward cyclical spiral. Ultimately, their rejection of God's word leads them to become worse than the nations they conquered. Israel's egregious sins demand God's judgment upon His people, and result in a longing for a good king to lead them to walk with God.

JUDGES 1:1–3:6: GOD LEAVES THE CANAANITES AS THORNS IN ISRAEL'S SIDE

God commands the tribe of Judah to lead the fight against the Canaanites, but Israel falters. Tribe by tribe, the Israelites break God's command. In response, God refuses to remove the Canaanites. Instead, they will be thorns in Israel's side to see if His people will obey Him. They do not. Israel sins repeatedly, so God continually appoints adversaries against them. In their agony, Israel cries to God, who raises up judges as temporary deliverers. Despite Israel's flaws, God's Spirit leads the judges to partially deliver Israel.

God's Refusal to Help Israel Conquer the Canaanites

When Israel stopped obeying God, He stopped their elimination of the Canaanites. He left the Canaanites to test Israel. Will they trust God through conflict and show the Canaanites who God is? God seeks to deliver both Israelites and Canaanites.

JUDGES 3:7–16:31: MANY JUDGES LEAD ISRAEL

God appoints Othniel as judge to answer Israel's cries under the reign of King Cushan-Rishathaim. God's Spirit leads Othniel to defeat this king, but Israel returns to sin. God then chooses a Moabite king, Eglon, as an adversary. Israel's next judge, Ehud, slays Eglon, but the Israelites continue to sin. Deborah, an Israelite prophetess who judges Israel, calls Barak to lead Israel. Together, they defeat the enemy army and celebrate their victory with a song that foretells how God will one day destroy all His enemies.

God approaches Gideon to judge Israel next, but he proves reluctant. Eventually, Gideon tears down the idol Baal's altar, so God compels the hesitant judge to lead an army against the nation Midian. In order that God might be shown as the reason for Gideon's triumph rather than

Gideon himself, God makes sure that Gideon's army is too small to win by human means. Then God deceives Midian, whose soldiers turn upon themselves, and defeats their army. Some Israelites seek to make Gideon king, but he rejects them, saying God is Israel's king. Moments later, however, Gideon fashions an idol, rejecting God's word. His idolatry influences the next generation to sin, especially when Gideon's illegitimate son, Abimelech, murders sixty-nine of his seventy half-brothers. The people of Shechem choose Abimelech as their king, but they turn on each other. Shechem seeks to replace Abimelech, who then traps Shechem's people in a tunnel and burns them alive. Abimelech finally dies when a woman at a tower drops a stone upon him.

After two more judges, Tola and Jair, Israel's sins only grow, as it waits for the next judge: Jephthah. By God's Spirit, Jephthah leads Israel in a great victory, but he also foolishly vows to devote the first thing out of his house to God. Unfortunately, his only child, his daughter, comes out. This hasty vow ends his family line, as she remains a virgin. Israel again falls into sin. God then exaults, or raises up, Ibzan, Elon, and Abdon to judge Israel.

In response to Israel's sin, God raises up the Philistines over Israel. He then promises a son, Samson, to an older, barren Israelite couple. God sets a lifetime Nazarite vow on Samson, meaning that he must not touch dead things, drink strong alcohol, or cut his hair. Through this vow, God's Spirit provides Samson amazing strength, but Samson repeatedly rejects God. Eventually, a Philistine woman uncovers that Samson's strength is from the vow. After she cuts his hair, the last part of the vow to be broken, the Philistines capture him and gouge out his eyes. In his blind imprisonment, Samson asks God to give him one more feat of strength because he finally sees how God is his strength. He stretches out his hands against the pillars of the house and crashes three thousand Philistines upon his own head, defeating them with his own death.

JUDGES 17:1–21:25: ISRAEL'S IDOLATRY WITHOUT JUDGES

A man named Micah builds an idol. He establishes his own approach to worshipping God and hires a Levite to serve as his priest, violating God's commands. When the tribe of Dan sees this Levite and the idol, they take them both for themselves.

Another Levite travels with his concubine as he passes through the Israelite town of Gibeah from the tribe of Benjamin. This town should be a place where God's people live rightly, but they do not. After an old man shelters this Levite in his house, the men of Gibeah seek to sodomize the Levite in homosexual rape. To protect himself, the cowardly Levite hands over his concubine to the men of Gibeah to rape her all night. He finds her dead in the morning, takes her body, and cuts it into twelve pieces to send to Israel's twelve tribes. He warns the rest of Israel of Gibeah's great evil, not seeing his own wickedness in how he treated his concubine in every moment of their relationship. Israel then orders the tribe of Benjamin to hand over Gibeah. The tribe refuses, and civil war ensues. On the third day of battle after great losses, Israel finally prevails. Benjamin is ruined.

Because of Israel's vow to not allow their daughters to marry the men of Benjamin, the tribe of Benjamin will not continue until the next generation. Benjamin and the rest of Israel lament, but Israel realizes that one city did not fight against Benjamin. Benjamin should take their women. When the tribe needs even more women, Israel invites Benjamin to seize the Israelite women dancing in front of the tabernacle. Israel has become one sinful, idolatrous nation that is worse than the Canaanites they removed from the land. Israel's evil yields a longing for a king who will do what is right and lead Israel to do the same.

Benjamin's Failures

One city in Benjamin becomes like Sodom, and all of Benjamin rallies against God to defend it. The people of Benjamin know of God yet reject the Torah. Benjamin is then under the ban like the Canaanites, but God's mercy delays death and keeps some alive. God judges so that He can save. Throughout the Bible, God works to save and to limit sin's consequences. Israel is not the hero; God is.

KEY TAKEAWAYS

Israel's time under the judges reflects a recurring cycle of sin that leaves Israel worse than the Canaanites. God keeps the Canaanites in the land to test Israel. They do not pass this test, so God answers Israel's sins with more afflictions. When Israel cries to God, however, He hears and appoints deliverers to save them. Despite Israel's many sins and those of their judges, God delivers them and delays their judgment. Israel becomes worse than Sodom at the book's end because every Israelite does his own will rather than God's. The only answer is waiting for God's King.

1 SAMUEL

Waiting for a King after God's Own Heart

> "Behold, to obey is better than sacrifice."
> —1 Samuel 15:22

The last judge, Samuel, proves to be faithful, leading God's people to repent and trust God as their king. However, when Samuel grows old, Israel desires a king like all the nations, a human king to fight wars for them. God appoints Saul from Benjamin as Israel's first king. He is what the Israelites want as a king, but he is not what they need. Saul repeatedly disobeys God, so God seeks a better king. Samuel then anoints David from Judah as the next king, but David must wait until Saul's death to reign. Although he has chances to harm Saul, David refuses to strike him. Unfortunately, jealous Saul seeks to kill David. As Saul works harder and harder to kill David, Saul's own sin puts his house to death without David raising a hand against him.

1 SAMUEL 1–8: SAMUEL AS ISRAEL'S LAST JUDGE

A barren woman, Hannah, begs God for a son and offers to give him back to God in a lifetime Nazarite vow. After hearing her case, Eli, the High Priest, blesses her and asks God to fulfill her request. God remembers her. She gives birth to a son, Samuel, and takes him back to the tabernacle to serve God after he is weaned. As she hands off

Samuel, Hannah sees the birth of her son as a preview of how God will save in the last days.

Hannah's Hope

Hannah longs for a son, but God closes her womb. After much affliction, Hannah's love for a son is tied to an increasing love for God. By asking for a son whom she will give back to God, Hannah shows her hope is in God who provides every good gift.

God admonishes Eli for not restraining his sons' egregious sins when they serve as priests. They constantly break Moses' commandments and bring God's Ark into battle. The enemy Philistines rout Israel and kill Eli's sons. The Philistines take the Ark, and Eli dies at hearing this news. The Philistines' joy of capturing the Ark turns to fear when God plagues them. They send the Ark back to Israel. Nonetheless, Israel laments because their enemies, the Philistines, rule them. Then Samuel judges the people of Israel. He calls them to repent, remove idols, and allow God to deliver them. Israel heeds Samuel, and God delivers them. Samuel's judgeship enthrones God as Israel's king for many years.

1 SAMUEL 9–15: THE BEGINNING OF SAUL'S REIGN AS KING

As Samuel ages, the people ask him to appoint a human king. God warns Israel that such kings will bring great costs. Kings will use their children and demand the best of their work and property. Despite the warning, they demand a human king. With this request, Israel rejects God as their king.

God chooses a man from Benjamin, Saul, as king. Although Saul is reluctant to take the role, his victory in battle establishes his rule. Samuel, however, warns Israel that they should not have chosen a king. Going forward, both the king and the people need to obey God.

As the war with the Philistines continues, Samuel commands Saul to wait for Samuel to make sacrifices before a battle. When Saul's soldiers begin to depart from their lines, impatient Saul performs the sacrifice on his own. When Samuel arrives, he rebukes Saul for not waiting. Samuel says that God will take Saul's kingdom and give it to a better man. In the meantime, the war continues. Saul's son Jonathan proves himself valuable to his father, winning a great victory. After the victory, Samuel commands Saul to place some of the Amalekites under the ban. Saul only partially obeys this order, leaving the Amalekite king and their best animals alive for sacrifices, so Samuel rebukes Saul for his disobedience. God desires obedience more than sacrifice and again rejects Saul as king.

1 SAMUEL 16–31: THE SLOW FALL OF SAUL AND THE SLOW RISE OF DAVID

God sends Samuel to the house of Jesse in Bethlehem to anoint the next king. Samuel anoints his youngest son, David, as the one who will be king one day. God's Spirit comes upon David and allows him to make music, comforting troubled Saul.

The Philistine war carries on, and the Philistine champion Goliath challenges any Israelite to face him alone in battle to determine the fate of the two peoples. Israel trembles, but David agrees to fight. With his sling and a rock, David slays Goliath, beheading him with his own sword. David leads Israel's army to a victory with the Philistines. Although

David remains extremely faithful to Saul, the king grows jealous of David. He tries many ways to end David's life but always fails.

Remarkably, Saul's son Jonathan develops a close friendship with David. Jonathan knows David will be king one day and promises to serve him. David flees Saul. After a stop at the tabernacle where the priests care for him, he escapes to the wilderness. In anger, Saul murders the priests for helping David and pursues David. Twice, David has a chance to harm Saul without immediate consequence, but David chooses to not hurt God's anointed king. In the wake of David's good intentions and Samuel's death, Saul relents from his pursuit. Nonetheless, David fears for his life and seeks shelter with a foreign king, but his commanders do not trust David. Returning home, David finds his family captured by Amalekites. He rescues his family and destroys some of Amalek.

Saul faces battle without the now-deceased Samuel, so he enlists a medium to consult dead Samuel. Samuel's spirit rebukes Saul. He and his sons will die. As the dead Samuel promised, the gentiles wound Saul. His fear of being tortured leads him to take his own life by his sword.

KEY TAKEAWAYS

Samuel's judgeship paves the way for Israel's first king, Saul, who reluctantly took the crown after Israel wanted a king. Saul rejects God's word repeatedly, and out of jealousy seeks to kill loyal David. David flees, and Saul pursues. David refuses to harm Saul, but Saul's many attempts to kill David and to reject God lead him to put an end to his own rule. While David continues to prevail over all of Israel's enemies, Saul dies in battle by his own hand. God is the one who raises up the poor and humbles the mighty. He gives victory to those who seek Him and wait for His King.

2 SAMUEL

Waiting for the Son of David

"I shall go to him, but he shall not return to me."
—2 Samuel 12:23

David becomes the king of his own tribe, Judah, but the other tribes initially follow Saul's son. David's rule over all of Israel starts with successes in conquering Jerusalem and bringing God's Ark to the city. David desires to build God a permanent home for the Ark, but God rejects this plan. God promises that the yet-to-be-born Son of David will build an everlasting house for God that will also be David's house in the end. He delights that this promised person will come from his family. David, however, quickly falls into sin, which his sons multiply. One of them seeks David's life and throne. After much suffering, David returns to rule. He and his sons have not lived lives that build an enduring house for God, but the promised Son of David and his everlasting house remain David's hope for life.

2 SAMUEL 1–6: THE RISE OF DAVID'S KINGDOM

An Amalekite who falsely claims to have killed Saul hands David his crown. David summarily executes him for striking God's anointed king. Grieving, David laments Saul's and Jonathan's deaths. David's tribe, Judah, anoints him as king, but the other tribes enthrone Saul's son

Ish-Bosheth (or Ishbosheth). In the civil war, Ish-Bosheth weakens, but David and the tribe of Judah strengthen. Two men slaughter Ish-Bosheth and bring David his head. David executes them in response.

All of Israel enthrones David as king, and he conquers Jerusalem. He desires God's Ark to join him, but his first effort ends in a man's death. After this delay and God's blessing, David rejoices as they bring God's Ark to Jerusalem.

2 SAMUEL 7–10: THE SON OF DAVID

While sitting on his throne, David realizes he should not have such a grand home while God's Ark dwells in tent curtains. The prophet Nathan encourages him to act on his good desire to build God a house, but God counters Nathan's instruction. David, like any man, cannot build a house to contain the infinite God, and He has not asked Israel to build such a house. God promises, instead, that He will continue to shepherd David. God will make a house for David through the Son of David. After David dies, God will establish the kingdom of one of his sons. This Son of David will build a house for God that will endure forever. He will be David's son and God's son. This promise arrives, however, with a tension because sin is part of the story.

Though this Son of David will Himself succeed without sinning, the anticipation of His future success will be explained through the author depicting Israel's many sins. Israel's story with God previews the Son of David's story with God, but where Israel fails, the Son of David will succeed. As Israel has failed to follow God, David's many sons will continually fail until they are exiled. Afterward, this promised Son of David will build a permanent place for man and God to live together: a house with God. When David dies, he will live there with God forever. God blesses David as a king of kings whose lands stretch out, whose armies prevail, and whose riches increase. David also blesses Jonathan's crippled son, Mephibosheth, bringing him into his house. God will take care of the broken families like Saul's.

2 SAMUEL 11–21: THE SLOW FALL OF DAVID'S HOUSE

David's life turns when he seduces Bathsheba, a wife of his soldier Uriah. When she becomes pregnant, David attempts to cover up his sin by trying to manipulate the soldier to lay with his wife. Uriah refuses. David sends Uriah back to battle and orders the army to abandon him mid-fight. In this way, David murders Uriah and marries Bathsheba, who gives birth to their child.

Shortly thereafter, Nathan informs David of a rich man who stole from a poor man. David demands judgment on him, but Nathan declares David to be that rich man. David immediately repents of his sins against Uriah, but God brings judgment while keeping His promise of the Son of David. After Bathsheba's baby dies, she gives birth to another son, Solomon. In total, four sons will die because of David's sin with Bathsheba. The house of David will turn on itself.

David's Failures

In 2 Sam 11–21, David's failures are center stage. These failures help us look beyond David and his flawed sons to the perfect Son of David. We hold out hope for the Son who has made an ordered house that even David can enjoy forever through repentance and faith.

David's son Amnon rapes his half-sister, Tamar. Her brother Absalom avenges his sister's rape by murdering Amnon. After Absalom flees his father, David, a wise woman convinces David to not lose two sons at once. Absalom persuades the people to prefer him as king. He crowns himself and marches to Jerusalem to take his father's throne. David flees, but he must abandon his counselor and God's Ark. David retreats to the wilderness as Absalom conquers Jerusalem. Absalom's best counselor recommends that he race after David, but David's counselor friend recommends a delayed attack. This delay saves David. When the battle ensues, David asks his commanders to not harm Absalom. In the fierceness of the fight, however, Absalom dies. When David hears of Absalom's death, he cries out for his dead son. David returns to Jerusalem a weakened king.

2 SAMUEL 22–24: THE SON OF DAVID IS DAVID'S HOPE

Despite his failures, David worships God in a song of deliverance and poem that underscore God as his rock and hope. When his pride leads David, however, to count his people in a census, God's wrath falls upon Jerusalem. David offers a sacrifice and turns God's wrath.

KEY TAKEAWAYS

David becomes king of Israel, conquers Jerusalem, and takes the Ark there. He wants to build a permanent home for the Ark, but God promises to build an everlasting house through the Son of David. David quickly falls into sin, which spreads to his sons. After much agony, the promise of the upcoming Son of David and His house stand as David's hope.

1 KINGS

Many Failed Kings and a Promising Prophet

"I have surely built thee an house to dwell in."
—1 Kings 8:13

1 Kings (and later 2 Kings) answers the key question from 2 Samuel 7: Who is the Son of David who will build an everlasting house with God? While the book begins with optimism that David's son Solomon might be this man, it also unveils his idolatrous failure. Solomon is not the promised Son of David. After Solomon's egregious sins and death, God divides the one nation of Israel into two nations. David's and Solomon's sons rule the southern kingdom, Judah, with the temple and Jerusalem as its capital. The northern tribes form their own kingdom, Israel. The story shines a light on the dark reality of Israel's increasing sin, but it also focuses on the hope that emerges after judgment.

1 KINGS 1–10: KING SOLOMON BUILDS THE TEMPLE

Adonijah, one of David's sons, prepares to be king, but David instead anoints Solomon as ruler. In fear, Adonijah makes his half-brother promise not to kill him. Solomon agrees to let him live if Adonijah remains faithful to him. Before his death, David pulls Solomon aside to instruct him to obey God's commands so that God may always keep his sons on his throne. David also counsels Solomon to judge the men he himself had failed to judge. After David's death, these men and Adonijah, who seeks Solomon's throne, find judgment for their treacheries.

God appears to Solomon and asks him what gift he wants. Solomon asks for wisdom to lead God's people, which God grants. He walks in God's wisdom, a trait of the promised person from the Torah. He also builds God's house, the temple, a trait of the Son of David. When Solomon dedicates this temple, he sacrifices many animals as God's priest, leads his people as His king, and speaks for God as His prophet. Solomon knows that this house cannot contain God, but the temple is a house of prayer and a reminder of God's promises to Abraham and David. God will hear in heaven and remember His promises. Israel will remember God and repent after they sin. After this dedication, God reminds Solomon he must obey Moses' laws. His kingdom grows and becomes extremely wealthy. He is a king of kings.

1 KINGS 11–16: SOLOMON'S FALL AND THE EARLY KINGS OF JUDAH AND ISRAEL

Solomon abandons God's wisdom. As he builds God's temple, Solomon also marries seven hundred foreign women and claims three hundred concubines, building houses for their gods. The wisest man who ever lived makes himself a fool by forgetting the Torah. These women turn Solomon's heart away from God. Because of God's promise to David, however, God does not tear away the kingdom in Solomon's days.

Seeing Solomon As a Flawed Person

The Bible portrays key people's successes as a model of the Messiah, as seen with Noah, David, and Solomon. In showing Solomon's many failures, however, the book allows us to understand the full story. We cannot and should not confuse Solomon with the Messiah.

After Solomon dies, God stirs up conflict with Solomon's son, Rehoboam, and his adversary, Jeroboam. The northern tribes under Jeroboam will submit to Rehoboam if he lowers their taxes, but he instead raises their taxes. In response, Jeroboam leads the northern tribes to form a new kingdom, known as the northern kingdom, Ephraim, or Israel. The kingdom continually sins against God. The sons of David, Solomon, and Rehoboam continue to rule in Jerusalem over Judah, also known as the southern kingdom.

The remainder of 1 Kings goes back and forth between events in these two kingdoms. Each king's rule includes an introduction explaining when the king's rule begins, the king's mother, and the king's relationship to God. All kings are compared to David, who is considered faithful because he repented when God's word through a prophet confronted him. The good kings struggle to get rid of idols, and the bad kings multiply idolatry. Each king's story ends with a brief conclusion that reminds the reader of official court records and the king who ruled after them.

Rehoboam's flawed reign, which leaves God's people divided into two competing kingdoms, gives way to his son Abijam and grandson Asa in Judah. In the north, Jeroboam establishes a new priesthood to keep his people away from Jerusalem and the temple. God eventually judges Jeroboam and establishes a new dynasty with the ascension of king Ahab and his wife, Jezebel, over Israel.

1 KINGS 17–22: THE PROPHET ELIJAH AND KING AHAB

Ahab and Jezebel multiply Israel's idolatry, so God sends the prophet Elijah to confront Ahab. By God's command, Elijah causes a three-year drought throughout Israel and eventually confronts Ahab directly. Elijah initiates a contest between himself as God's prophet and the false prophets. When Elijah calls to God, He throws down fire from heaven. The people see that God is God and that the other prophets are false. After Elijah kills the false prophets, Jezebel threatens to murder him. In fear of her wrath, Elijah flees to Mount Sinai. Though he has commanded great power through God, Elijah's fear of her and his despair over people not stopping their idolatry overtakes him. At Mount Sinai, Elijah feels as though he is God's last follower. God sends Elijah back to Israel, giving him the younger prophet Elisha to help him, along with the encouragement that seven thousand other Israelites remain faithful. Elijah is not alone—God is with him.

Elijah's Failures

Elijah flees Jezebel's wrath, but God does not abandon the struggling Elijah. God sends him to Mount Sinai into the same situation that Moses faced. His life resembles that of Moses, which reminds the reader that we are waiting for the Prophet Like Moses. Elijah is not this promised person, however, because he is also unable to solve the problem of human death in God's presence.

Back in Israel, Elijah rebukes Ahab after he steals a vineyard from another man. Surprisingly, Ahab repents. Ahab then partners with the new king of Judah, Jehoshaphat, to join him in war, but the prophet Micaiah warns Ahab of his pending death in battle. Although Ahab tries to avoid dying, an archer's arrow slays him. His son Ahaziah becomes Israel's new king.

KEY TAKEAWAYS

While 1 Kings begins with the optimism that Solomon might be the Son of David, time unveils his idolatrous failure. He is not the promised Son of David. After Solomon's egregious sins and death, God divides the one nation into two nations: Israel and Judah. Most of these kings fail to follow God, but God raises prophets to call Israel in the north and Judah in the south to follow Him. The most significant of these prophets is Elijah, who confronts evil king Ahab with his idolatry.

2 KINGS

God's Patient Judgment of Israel and Judah

"Yet the LORD testified against Israel, and against Judah, by all the prophets."
—2 Kings 17:13

2 Kings picks up directly from where 1 Kings leaves off. Israel and Judah's kings struggle to follow God, making it clear that none of them are the Son of David. The prophetic work of Elijah ends, which begins the work of his great successor, Elisha. Elisha performs twice as many miracles as Elijah. After Elisha's ministry to Israel's kings ends in Elijah's own death, Ahab's dynasty falls in the north from its pervasive idolatry. The same sins occur in Judah partially due to intermarriage with Ahab's family. God summons the nation of Assyria to exile the northern kingdom of Israel because of its widespread idolatry. When Assyria fails to conquer Judah, God uses kings Hezekiah and Josiah to lead Judah well. After Josiah's reign ends, however, God calls the nation of Babylon to judge Judah for rampant idolatry. He sends Judah to exile, leaving Jerusalem and the temple in ruins.

2 KINGS 1–17: THE PROPHETS AND KINGS UNTIL ASSYRIA CONQUERS ISRAEL

Elisha follows the elder prophet Elijah closely as he parts the Jordan River, leading Elisha through the water. Elisha asks Elijah for a double portion of his spirit—he desires to let God's Spirit lead him to perform more miracles and surpass Elijah's ministry. God sends a fiery chariot that takes Elijah up to heaven. Elisha picks up Elijah's staff and coat and parts the river himself. Elisha continues and expands his ministry, performing twice as many miracles. God shows patience and mercy with Israel through Elisha, but ultimately, God exalts Jehu to end the rule of Ahab's family in the north. He also slays Judah's king, also named Ahaziah, whose mother, Athaliah, is from Ahab's family.

To gain power as queen of Judah, Athaliah murders all her grandsons in Judah except one, Joash, who is hidden from her in the temple. When the priests bring Joash forward as heir, they lead Jerusalem to execute Athaliah. Joash rules well for a time, but he, too, dies. Several kings lead Judah after this point, and Israel's sins increase. God judges the northern kingdom Israel for its idolatry and lack of faith in God's prophets. He summons the nation of Assyria to exile Israel. Judah continues to fall prey to the same idolatries, for which God judged the now-defunct northern kingdom.

2 KINGS 18:1–23:30: KINGS HEZEKIAH AND JOSIAH OF JUDAH

After conquering Israel, Assyria surrounds Jerusalem, which is currently under the rule of King Hezekiah. Hezekiah trusts in God unlike any other Judean king before or after. With the city surrounded by the Assyrian army, the Assyrian spokesman warns the Israelites to not trust Hezekiah and God. Hezekiah turns to God. He prays, and God answers through Isaiah, God's prophet. Jerusalem will be delivered, and the Assyrian army will be defeated. Although the city seemed destined to die, it finds life. God's angel kills the army, and the Assyrian king returns home only to be murdered by his own sons.

Hezekiah also trusts God when Isaiah warns him that he will die from sickness. The beleaguered king prays to God and asks to extend his life. God adds fifteen more years of life. During that time, Hezekiah shows his kingdom's treasuries to Babylonian envoys. Isaiah declares that after Hezekiah's days Babylon will tear down the kingdom, loot its treasures, and send the people and his sons into exile in Babylon. Hezekiah hears God's word from the prophet and confirms God's goodness because he sees God being patient with him and his kingdom.

Hezekiah's son, Manasseh, becomes king and leads Israel into unprecedented amounts of idolatry. Manasseh murders his own children to worship Canaanite idols and gods. He sets carved images of the foreign gods within God's temple. God then declares that Judah's pending exile is now unavoidable. His son, Amon, proves no better, and his short reign ends with his eight-year-old son, Josiah, becoming king.

Hezekiah's and Josiah's Failures

There was no king like Hezekiah or Josiah. They were superlative, but neither could pass on an enduring throne or turn God's wrath so that His people might dwell with Him. Someone greater than Hezekiah and Josiah will be needed: the Son of David.

Eighteen years later, Josiah decides to repair the temple. When his subjects begin work, however, they find a lost book in the temple. It is Moses' book, the Torah. As they read the book to King Josiah, he recognizes his sin and repents. Josiah learns that Judah will soon face God's judgment, but because of his repentance God delays judgment until after Josiah's death. Josiah leads the whole nation to hear the Torah and to renew itself to God. Josiah removes many idols and reclaims parts of the now-exiled northern kingdom. He loves God unlike any of Judah's kings before or after him. Despite all that Josiah does, even he cannot turn God's wrath. This means that someone greater than even Josiah or Hezekiah will have to come to turn God's wrath: the Son of David. Josiah ultimately dies in battle, and the people set Jehoahaz as king.

2 KINGS 23:31–25:30: BABYLON AND THE LAST KINGS OF JUDAH

Jehoahaz reigns over Israel for a mere three months before Jehoiakim takes his place. God then commands Babylon to judge Judah during Jehoiakim's reign. Upon Jehoiakim's death, Jehoiachin reigns for three months. King Nebuchadnezzar of Babylon then marches upon Jerusalem and takes Jehoiachin and many others into exile. Nebuchadnezzar sets another king on the throne: Zedekiah.

Zedekiah rebels against Babylon's king. The Babylonians eventually capture him, slaughter his sons, burn down the temple, and destroy Jerusalem's walls. They send even more of Judah's people into exile. Finally, Babylon sets a governor over Jerusalem and Judah, Gedaliah. The remaining people in the land murder Gedaliah and flee to Egypt. Yet, God watches over Jehoiachin in his exile. The Babylonian king shows Jehoiachin mercy, sustains him at his table, and sets him above the other kings for the rest of his life.

KEY TAKEAWAYS

God answers His people's idol worship with His prophets, Moses' book, and distant nations. After Israel's exile to Assyria, Hezekiah and Josiah rule Judah by faith in God, but they cannot turn God's wrath. God sends Babylon to exile Jerusalem and Judah, but He comforts King Jehoiachin in exile. The reader is subtly reminded that God will keep His promise to David. The Prophet's search for the Messiah continues, looking for someone greater than Moses, Joshua, David, Solomon, Elijah, Elisha, Hezekiah, and Josiah.

ISAIAH

Who Is the Son of David and What Will He Do?

"Behold, a virgin shall conceive, and bear a son, and shall call his name Immanuel."
—Isaiah 7:14

Isaiah explains Israel's and Judah's exiles by reminding us of the promises of Moses' final poems in Deuteronomy 32 and 33. The first third of Isaiah wrestles with the identity of the promised deliverer, Immanuel, whose name means "God with us." This man, born of a virgin, will be the Son of David. He will redeem and ransom a people for Himself, leading people from all nations and generations to Jerusalem to worship God. The middle third of Isaiah covers Isaiah's ministry to Hezekiah. The book's final third explains what the Son of David will do when He comes. Immanuel will offer Himself as an atoning sacrifice that will turn God's wrath. This Messiah will soften the hearts of the very people who afflicted Him. They will become God's people through Immanuel's work.

ISAIAH 1–12: THE PROMISE OF IMMANUEL FOR ISRAEL

God's sinful people are rejecting Him. No matter what God does, they rebel. He tells them to repent and promises to cleanse them in the end. The prophet Isaiah sees God in a vision. God's voice shakes the heavenly temple, and the prophet fears his death in God's presence. God asks who will proclaim His message to Israel. Isaiah agrees without hesitation to speak for God. Israel will reject Isaiah's words because no matter what God does or says, they will not hear, understand, or believe. Isaiah will carry out God's message until Israel is in exile.

Isaiah approaches Judah's king Ahaz and commands the king to ask God for a sign, but Ahaz tests God by refusing His command. God promises a sign. "Behold, a virgin shall conceive, and bear a son, and shall call his name Immanuel" (Isa 7:14). Who is this son, Immanuel? His name means "God with us." Immanuel will sit on David's throne as God's king in an everlasting kingdom. He will be the promised Son of David. Immanuel will have God's Spirit, will delight in God, and will rule righteously by the word of His mouth. His word will change the whole creation, everything that exists, and yield a highway for God's people to return to Him from exile.

Who Is Immanuel?

The author clarifies in Isaiah 9 and 11 that Immanuel will be God Himself and the Son of David, not the other sons named in the book, such as Shear Yashub (or Shearjashub) and Maher-Shalal-Hashbaz (or Mahershalalhashbaz). His kingdom will never end, so Hezekiah cannot be Immanuel. Immanuel will come in the last days.

ISAIAH 13–23: THE PROMISE OF IMMANUEL FOR ALL NATIONS

Isaiah brings God's word to the nations, drawing out implications of Immanuel's identity for the peoples. Just as God rebukes Israel's sin, the sins of many other nations will bring God's wrath. These nations also need to repent before the Son of David comes. Most importantly, the scattering of God's people among the nations will bring God's word to them. In the end, the nations will walk with Israel back to God. They will be a part of God's people streaming back to Jerusalem on His highway. The nations will be part of an Israel that will be more than just Israel.

ISAIAH 24–35: THE PROMISE OF IMMANUEL FOR ALL GENERATIONS

The judgments of Canaan are a preview of God's last judgment of all of His creation. The old creation will die as God's kingdom approaches, and God's rule will bring new life in a new creation. In the end, God will rule as king with His glory on display everywhere. Immanuel will rule righteously. God's appearance and vengeance will bring life to the dead places and hope to God's redeemed and ransomed people. His people will return to Jerusalem on God's holy highway with great singing and celebration.

ISAIAH 36–39: WAITING FOR IMMANUEL'S DAYS

Unlike his father, Ahaz, Hezekiah turns to God and trusts Him when his city, kingdom, and his own body seem as good as dead. When Assyria surrounds Jerusalem with a massive army, God saves the city through Hezekiah's prayer. When Hezekiah is gravely ill, God extends his life fifteen more years. When Hezekiah shows the treasures of the temple to the Babylonians, Isaiah proclaims that the Babylonians will be the ones to take this treasure from the temple after his days. Hezekiah affirms God's good word because "there shall be peace and truth in my days" (Isaiah 39:8).

ISAIAH 40–55:
WHAT IMMANUEL WILL DO

The last third of the book promises compassion for God's people. Isaiah declares that a voice crying in the wilderness, a prophet, will prepare the way for the coming of God's Kingdom to the earth. Throughout four "servant songs," Isaiah details what the Son of David will do. The Son of David will be the Suffering Servant who will have God's Spirit, bring forth God's justice to the nations, and find faraway nations seeking His instruction. All will learn that God is the only Savior. Kings and peoples will respond to the Son of David. This Suffering Servant will not appear distinguished, but He will bear the sins of God's people, who will be known not by their ethnicity but by their repentance. The judgment for all of their sins will be laid on this one man, whose atoning sacrificial death will turn God's wrath. God will be pleased by this act, and many people will join Him in life after death. The Suffering Servant, Immanuel, will turn rebellious people into God's people.

The Suffering Servant

The Suffering Servant will live among His people but will be very different from them. He will endure the death God's people deserve so that they can repent and trust Him. His sacrificial death will turn God's wrath, please God, and bring God's everlasting life everywhere.

ISAIAH 56–66: WHAT IMMANUEL WILL CREATE

The sacrifice of the Suffering Servant will create a new heaven and earth. The arrival of God with man when this Messiah comes will bring salvation to all who heed His voice. God's people will be revealed when He arrives to judge and save. His new creation will reflect God's goodness on earth as it is in heaven. God's people will rejoice as His servants, worshipping Him forever. Those who oppose Him will face everlasting judgment.

KEY TAKEAWAYS

God proclaims Immanuel's identity as the Son of David, who will redeem and ransom God's people. He will be born of a virgin and lead people from all nations to worship God. God's word will be heard everywhere. Immanuel will be a Suffering Servant who will offer Himself as an atoning sacrifice so that God may delight in His Son. His death will turn the hearts of the very people who afflicted Him to repent and delight in Him forever.

JEREMIAH

The Weeping Prophet

> "I have this day set thee over the nations and over the kingdoms, to root out, and to pull down, and to destroy, and to throw down, to build, and to plant."
> —Jeremiah 1:10

The book of Jeremiah explains Moses' last major speech in Deuteronomy 29–30. The book promises both judgment and salvation for God's people in the last days. The prophet Jeremiah warns Judah and its kings that God will send them into exile, but the people and their false prophets reject this counsel. God confirms Jeremiah's words, however, as He summons Babylon to conquer Jerusalem, exile many people, and destroy the temple. Because Jeremiah's judgment was confirmed, the reader trusts Jeremiah's words of God's future salvation of His people. God will overturn Israel's and Judah's captivity.

JEREMIAH 1: THE PROPHET'S CALL

In the final years of Judah, God calls young Jeremiah to speak as His prophet to the nations. God sets His words in Jeremiah's mouth so that they might pluck up, break down, destroy, and throw down the world's kingdoms. This destruction will allow God to build and plant His own Kingdom. God will watch over Jeremiah's ministry to accomplish His will through His word. God will raise up a distant nation to judge His own people.

The Only Salvation Is Through God

Jeremiah preaches God's commands that move from judgment of our sin to salvation in our repentance and faith in Him. God's word comes to people as we are, complete with our sins and flaws. What we desire is insufficient to give lasting life, but what God desires is sufficient so that we can live with Him. Trusting God is the only way to true salvation.

JEREMIAH 2–25: GOD JUDGES HIS PEOPLE

Jeremiah presents God's case against His people. God provides them with blessings and life with Him, but they exchange God's glory for mere idols. Yet God still offers the people of Israel and Judah life through repentance and a return to Him. He elevates the nation of Babylon to bring calamity on His people so they return to Him in genuine humility and trust His word.

Judah's false prophets reject Jeremiah's counsel. They find safety in the presence of God's temple, rather than in obedience to God's word. Jeremiah warns them that if God destroyed the place of the tabernacle, the place of the temple may also be judged. God's presence invites His judgment as well as His blessing. Judah's leaders and people need to repent, obey God's voice, and learn to boast about God, not simply His temple. God brings Babylon to judge Judah and Jerusalem so that they will learn how powerless their idols are. God sends His people into exile because of the hardness of their hearts. In the last days, the Son of David will come to lead God's people and all nations in righteousness. God's future salvation will be greater than what He did for Israel in Egypt, but Judah will go into exile under Babylon for seventy years.

The Instant Gratification of Idolatry

Judah struggles with idols because all people desire what is immediate and tangible. Idols always promise the "now," but they will lead to sin and destruction. God guarantees the end and promises to sustain a person until then.

JEREMIAH 26–35: GOD GIVES HOPE TO HIS PEOPLE

God's people must respond to God's word in order to live, because God is coming to judge them, the temple, and Jerusalem. The leaders and false prophets struggle against God's word from Jeremiah, arguing that Judah's forced exile will be short. Jeremiah drafts a letter to those in exile and warns them that they will be exiled by Babylon for seventy years. God's people must seek the good of their enemies in the place of their exile. When seventy years are completed for Babylon, God will overturn His people's captivity in exile. God's plan for Israel is good. While exiled, His people will repent and seek God with all their hearts.

Jeremiah explains this future return to God and overturning of Judah's captivity that will happen in the last days. God will make a new covenant with His people. He will set His laws in their hearts, and their sins will be forgiven. God tells Jeremiah to buy land in the face of judgment because after judgment and exile will be a return from exile, eternal life, and hope.

JEREMIAH 36–45: GOD'S PEOPLE OPPOSE JEREMIAH

Jeremiah writes a scroll that is read to King Jehoiakim. Jehoiakim burns the scroll. Jeremiah dictates a new scroll with the same words with some additional content. As King Nebuchadnezzar's army approaches the city, Jerusalem's angry leaders throw Jeremiah into a pit with no water. The prophet rebukes and warns Judah's king before Babylon enters Jerusalem, captures and blinds the king, and executes his sons. Jeremiah counsels the remaining people to stay under the Babylonians who now rule Jerusalem with a puppet king, Gedaliah. Gedaliah is assassinated by some of the rebels, but Jeremiah calls them again to submit to Babylon, stay in the land, and avoid going down to Egypt. Rejecting Jeremiah's word, they flee to Egypt and take Jeremiah with them by force.

JEREMIAH 46–51: GOD JUDGES THE NATIONS

God judges the surrounding nations for their sins against God. They have the same sins as Israel and the same hope. Throughout repeated outcries against sin and warnings of judgment, God promises that He will overturn the captivity and restore the fortunes of Moab, Ammon, and Elam, just as He will for Israel. Jeremiah's helper, Seraiah, proclaims God's judgment on Babylon from Jeremiah's scroll. When finished reading, Seraiah takes the scroll and ties it to a stone that he drops into the Euphrates River. As the scroll sinks to the bottom, Babylon will do the same.

JEREMIAH 52: BABYLON DESTROYS JERUSALEM

The author flashes back to the Babylonian conquest of Jerusalem, confirming that Jeremiah's words of judgment to pluck up, break down, destroy, and throw down were true. The reader can trust that His words of hope to rebuild are also true. God's mercy on the exiled king of Judah, King Jehoiachin, one of David's descendants, reminds us that God will sustain His people until they return to Him.

KEY TAKEAWAYS

Jeremiah warns Judah and its kings that God will send them into exile for their idolatry, but they reject his counsel. God confirms Jeremiah's words as He raises up Babylon to conquer Jerusalem, exile many people, and destroy the temple. As Jeremiah's words of judgment ring true, the reader hopes for a future when God will overturn Israel's and Judah's captivity.

EZEKIEL

Visions of God

> "A new heart also will I give you, and a new spirit will I put within you: and I will take away the stony heart out of your flesh, and I will give you an heart of flesh."
> —Ezekiel 36:26

During Judah's final days, God speaks to the prophet Ezekiel while he is in exile. He provides him with visions of Himself that startle the reader. The opening vision establishes God's presence and explains why God judges the idolatry of His people and their temple. God's glory will depart from them so that in the end, He may return to them and all nations. In this return, God promises a final time when man will have renewed hearts to love God. Ezekiel promises His coming Kingdom's future arrival in a new King, a new land, a new temple, and a new city.

EZEKIEL 1–3: GOD CALLS EZEKIEL TO SPEAK TO ISRAEL

While the prophet and priest Ezekiel is among Judah's exiled people, God appears to him in a prophetic vision. God arrives in a dramatic whirlwind, a terrifying chaos with a series of cherubim, angelic beings, that dart to and fro. Their winged movements veil God and herald His voice. Above them, God sits on a throne with dazzling lights emanating from Him: the likeness of God's glory.

God's Cherubim

The Torah and the Prophets define most of God's angelic beings as cherubim. The cherubim guard the way back to the tree of life and God's presence in Genesis 3. They block the complete sight of God and proclaim His voice, as they do here in Ezekiel.

God's Spirit lifts Ezekiel. Ezekiel is directed to speak God's word to those with hardened hearts. Within this vision, God asks Ezekiel to eat a scroll filled with bitter words that become sweet. The prophet must proclaim God's message to the exiles for seven days. God's people are stunned as Ezekiel and his words grieve and upset them. Because they are a rebellious house who will not listen to Ezekiel's words, God closes His prophet's mouth so he cannot speak.

EZEKIEL 4–7: EZEKIEL WARNS OF JERUSALEM'S PENDING DESTRUCTION

God commands the temporarily muted Ezekiel to declare His word through prophetic actions. Among these signs, Ezekiel eats defiled bread baked on manure and shaves his hair and beard. He burns and scatters the hair, but he saves a remnant of it as God will save a remnant of His people out of judgment. Some of God's people will have confidence in Him during their exile and survive judgment.

EZEKIEL 8–12: EZEKIEL'S VISION OF GOD'S GLORY DEPARTING THE TEMPLE AND JERUSALEM

Within a vision, God brings Ezekiel to Jerusalem's temple, unveiling its overwhelming number of idols. God calls His angelic executioners to judge the city, with the last of these angelic beings writing God's word. Within this vision, His messengers mark those who grieve over idolatry so that they will be spared. Everything and everyone else will be destroyed. As the vision continues, the cherubim remove the Ark and carry it away to the east. After this promise of future judgment and destruction, God's people will one day receive a new heart from Him, a changed heart that loves God completely, so that they will reject idols.

EZEKIEL 13–24: EZEKIEL PROMISES JUDGMENT

False prophets wrongly claim that peace awaits God's people rather than suffering and exile. God has blessed Israel with His presence, but they continue to spurn His word. Yet Ezekiel sees hope in their exile. From there, God will return His people to Him.

EZEKIEL 25–32: EZEKIEL PROMISES JUDGMENT ON THE SURROUNDING NATIONS

Starting with two nations that descend from Lot's family, Ammon and Moab, God promises that all nations will face His judgment. Even the descendants of Esau, which is the nation Edom, and the neighboring Philistines will find judgment. These nations tempt God's people to sin and worship idols, especially Tyre, which the King James Version archaically spells *Tyrus*, and its king. Ezekiel compares the king of Tyre's temptation of His people to what the serpent did in the garden to Adam and Eve. Sidon, which the King James Version archaically spells *Zidon*, and Egypt will find judgment so that they, too, may know who God is.

EZEKIEL 33–48: EZEKIEL PROMISES FUTURE BLESSING FOR ISRAEL

As the news of Jerusalem's destruction comes to Ezekiel, God opens his mouth to rebuke Israel's leaders for the mistreatment of God's people. God will be their shepherd. He will save His scattered flock through the Son of David. Edom, and every person who will not follow the Son of David, will find their kingdoms and mountains destroyed when God's Kingdom comes. God will, however, bless Israel's mountains. He will show compassion to His people. As He scattered them, God will also return them. His people will return to

Him because God will change their hearts to love Him and reject idols. God's Spirit will be put within them.

In a vision, God shows Ezekiel a valley of dry bones. God's word and Spirit bring life to these bones, as He will give life to the dead Israelites in the end. His Spirit will live in them. In the last days, the nations will oppose God's people, but God will restore His people's fortunes and overturn their captivity. In the end, all nations will see God's glory in how He saves His people who will have God's Spirit poured out on them.

God then offers visions of a new temple under the Son of David. The author unveils this perfect new temple to humble His people so that they may be ashamed of their sin and ponder the righteousness of God's coming Kingdom. God's renewed people will fill the whole promised land, especially the city where God dwells.

KEY TAKEAWAYS

God provides Ezekiel, who is in exile, with visions of Himself. He desires for His people to live with Him so that His glory may reach beyond them to all nations. While the temple that Solomon built is now filled with many idols, God promises both judgment and exile. He promises a final time when man will have renewed hearts to love God and live with Him forever. Ezekiel promises God's coming Kingdom by speaking of the Son of David, the promised land renewed, the perfect temple, and the city where righteousness dwells.

THE TWELVE MINOR PROPHETS, PART 1

Hosea, Joel, Amos, and Obadiah

> "And it shall come to pass, that whosoever shall call
> on the name of the LORD shall be delivered."
> —Joel 2:32

The ending of the Prophets contains twelve books designed to be read as one book: aptly named the Book of the Twelve. This book begins with Hosea, Joel, Amos, and Obadiah. In Hosea, God uses a broken marriage to depict Israel's idolatry against God and how He will save His people. Joel then considers God's coming army, which will destroy sin in the promised land in the day of the LORD. Those who repent will receive His Spirit and find themselves renewed by God's presence. Next, Amos judges Israel for sinning like all the other nations. They will meet God's judgment, but God will restore His people's fortunes and overturn their captivity (return them from exile). Finally, Obadiah explains the judgment of the nation of Edom as a preview of the judgment of all nations.

HOSEA

God calls the prophet Hosea to marry a prostitute, Gomer, and have children who will follow her example. God teaches about Israel's idolatries against God through this troubled union. Gomer's unfaithfulness to Hosea reflects Israel's unfaithfulness to God. Their children's names map out God's plan to save people through His judgment:

- The oldest is named Jezreel, which means "God will sow." God is sowing judgment in response to Israel's many sins.
- The second child is named Lo-Ruhamah (or Loruhamah), which means "No compassion." God's judgment will remove His compassion for Israel. God's compassionate action is to remove His compassion in exile, so that Israel may return and receive His compassion in the end.
- The third child is named Lo-Ammi (or Loammi), which means "Not my people." When God removes His compassion from Israel, they will be like the rest of the nations in exile.

Despite this coming exile and judgment, God promises that Israel will eventually return to God. Those who repent will become His people and find His compassion because God sows judgment for the sake of salvation.

Hosea rebukes Israel's idolatries. They are like the other nations, who have stubborn hearts and commit evil. Echoing Adam, Israel is breaking God's covenant and will face exile because they need to repent. Hosea finds Israel's future hope embedded in Israel's past. Just as God ushered Israel out of Egypt in Moses' days, so God will call the Son of David and His people out of Egypt in the last days. If Israel repents, He will heal their apostasy (their turning away from Him). Only those who are wise will realize that God's words and ways are right and follow them.

JOEL

The prophet Joel asks the elders, or the older men, of Israel to look carefully for what God says will come in the end. It will not be found in the past or the present, so the wise man will keep talking about God's word to later generations to prepare for the day of the LORD, the last day of God's judgment. He describes this last judgment as a devastating locust invasion and conquest by an overwhelming foreign army.

The Day of the LORD

Many of the prophets promise God's final judgment on the day of the LORD, or the last day of the last days. When God's kingdom completely arrives, God will eliminate all idols, put to death the old creation, and unveil the new heavens and the earth.

Joel goes on to explain that God will shake the comfort of His people suddenly. They should repent now because the day of the LORD draws near. These promised locust and army invasions will devastate the land and the people, but those who repent will find a renewed life in God. God promises to pour out His Spirit on all His people, even as the entire creation faces death in God's presence. Everyone who calls on God's name will be saved. God will restore the fortunes of His people and overturn their exile in the sight of the nations that gather for war against His people. God's voice will roar from Mount Zion; namely, from Jerusalem where God dwells, against all those who oppose Him. In the end, the promised land will flow with God's life because He will dwell with His people on Mount Zion.

AMOS

God's voice roars from Zion against the sin of all nations. Through Amos, God rebukes Israel's and Judah's neighbors before turning to admonish His people. They are sinning like the rest of the nations, and they will soon meet God's face in judgment. God confronts Israel with three major sins: injustice, hypocrisy, and arrogance. Because the day of the LORD (the last day of God's judgment) is coming, God's people must repent or face His wrath.

Amos receives three initial visions of God's pending judgment on Israel: a locust invasion, a fiery judgment, and a plumb line, which speaks of measuring the city for judgment from God. Because of Amos's intercession, God delays judgment via the locusts and fire. However, the time to measure and judge Israel's idolatry has come. God will send Israel into exile, so He answers their continual sin and the time of judgment with a fourth vision, a vision of a summer basket, which warns the time is ripe for God's judgment. However, in his fifth vision, God promises life during judgment through the Son of David. God's people will possess what remains of Edom and all the nations when God restores the fortunes of His people and overturns their captivity from exile.

Restoring the Fortunes and Overturning Captivity

The prophets read Deuteronomy closely and trust its promise of God restoring the fortunes of His people and overturning their captivity in Deuteronomy 30:3. After the pain of exile, God's compassion will accompany His people's return to God's in the last days.

OBADIAH

Obadiah rebukes the nation of Edom. As Israel derives from Jacob, so Edom descends from Jacob's brother, Esau. The nation Edom has afflicted its brother nation, Israel, and will be covered in shame for not helping them. They gloated and mocked Israel, but the day of the LORD awaits not only them but all nations. As all people have done to others, so it will be done to them. Those who reject the promised Son of David's house will find judgment and death, but those who seek refuge in the Son of David will rule over all the mountains because the remaining Kingdom will be God's.

KEY TAKEAWAYS

Hosea, Joel, Amos, and Obadiah begin the Book of the Twelve. Hosea's faithfulness to his adulteress wife teaches about God's faithfulness to unfaithful Israel. Joel promises God destroying sin in the land in the day of the LORD. Repentant ones will receive His Spirit and be renewed by God's presence. Amos judges Israel for sinning like all the other nations. Still, after judgment, God will restore His people's fortunes and overturn their captivity from exile. God's people will possess the remnant of Edom and all nations. Finally, Obadiah explains the judgment of Edom as a preview of all nations' judgment.

THE TWELVE MINOR PROPHETS, PART 2

Jonah, Micah, Nahum, Habakkuk, and Zephaniah

"Therefore I will look unto the LORD;
I will wait for the God of my salvation: my God will hear me."
—Micah 7:7

The Twelve continues with Jonah, Micah, Nahum, Habakkuk, and Zephaniah. Jonah rejects God's word, but His patience with Jonah means that some gentiles trust God and become His priests and people. Micah answers Israel's sin with hope that God Himself will arrive as His people's King. Nahum rebukes Nineveh, the capital city of Assyria that exiled the northern kingdom, for its sin because God's vengeance and compassion arrive together when God's Kingdom will end all human kingdoms. In Habakkuk, God answers Jerusalem's sins by choosing the wicked Babylonians to judge them. Finally, Zephaniah understands the day of the LORD as the time when God will judge the whole creation so that He may restore the fortunes of His people and overturn their captivity.

JONAH

God calls the prophet Jonah to preach against Nineveh. He flees this call and instead boards a ship headed in the opposite direction. God hurls a great storm against the ship, which leads its gentile sailors to ask Jonah about his God. The captain of the sailors hopes that God's concern for them will keep them from perishing. Jonah warns them that God is judging them because he is fleeing God. They must hurl him into the sea to stop the storm, but they refuse to harm him until no other option remains. They pray to God and heed the prophet's word, hurling Jonah into the seas. As the storm calms, these sailors fear God and offer Him vows and sacrifices as His priests. God sends a large fish to swallow Jonah, who then realizes his sin and calls to God from the depths of the water. Salvation is from God, and Jonah will fulfill his vow. God commands the fish to vomit the prophet onto the dry land.

Jonah As God's Rebellious Prophet

It can be difficult to root for Jonah when comparing him to the other prophets. His book is mostly narrative and not poetry, and he willingly rejects God's word twice. He was not a good prophet by any measure, but he is not the story's hero—God is.

God calls Jonah a second time to preach against Nineveh. God will wipe out the city in forty days. When this word reaches Nineveh's king, he calls everyone to repent so God may show mercy and not kill them. God sees their repentance and delays His wrath, but Jonah becomes angry for God's compassion on them. Jonah knew God would show Nineveh the same mercy He showed Israel at Mount Sinai. God appoints a plant to comfort the beleaguered prophet with shade from the heat, but He also destroys it. Answering Jonah's next wave of anger, God asks the prophet if He should show the same mercy to Nineveh that Jonah and Israel receive. The book rebukes Jonah for not showing the compassion he received from God.

MICAH

The prophet Micah calls all peoples to prepare for the coming of God's Kingdom, when He will overturn all of creation. The nations see God exile His people, their presumed enemy, but they should not rejoice, because judgment awaits all peoples. God will return waves of His people to the land as their King. In the last days, peoples from all nations will stream to Jerusalem because the Torah will go out from Jerusalem to every nation. This King will be God Himself, and He will be born in Bethlehem.

In the end, Israel will want to do what God requires. They will walk humbly with God, practicing justice and loving-kindness. The nation must endure God's wrath because of its sin, but His people will see God's salvation. As God led them out of Egypt, God will save them so that the nations may also fear Him. God's past salvation previews His future salvation. He will pass over and forgive His people's rebellion. His wrath will end because God delights in unchanging love, according to His promise to Abraham.

NAHUM

The prophet Nahum describes the beauty of God's patient and complete judgment of all sin so that humankind may live. He sees God's Kingdom coming to destroy all of creation. He knows that no person can stand in the presence of God's wrath, but he also believes God will be a refuge in His wrath for those who trust Him. Nineveh will face God's judgment and complete destruction. The strength of the people of Nineveh will vanish, but God Himself will restore Israel's beauty. The contrast is clear. Nineveh's wealth, rulers, and people will lie dead and scattered. They have no remedy except seeking God. All the nations that Nineveh has cruelly sinned against will applaud God's judgment.

HABAKKUK

The prophet Habakkuk sees God's people in Jerusalem rejecting the Torah, so God appoints the cruel Babylonians to judge them. Habakkuk questions God's plan: How can God use a nation that slaughters others without mercy? God commands him to write down and read His response and vision to others. God delays His judgment, but His people should wait for it. It will not be late. His judgment divides all people into either the proud or the righteous, who live by his faith. Judgment awaits all who afflict others, so all peoples should be silent in His presence. Habakkuk praises God. He knows that he must endure God's wrath, but He will still worship God despite losing everything.

ZEPHANIAH

Zephaniah views Jerusalem's coming judgment as a preview of God's last judgment on all of creation. He employs the Torah's images of the flood in Noah's day to proclaim the coming of the day of the LORD. Humble people must seek God so that He may heal them on the day of His anger. His judgment and salvation will, in the end, leave behind God's people as humble and lowly. He will give His exiled people renown and praise when He restores their fortunes and overturns their captivity.

KEY TAKEAWAYS

These books in the Twelve show us how God brings judgment to Israel and the nations so that His people—who will come from all nations—may worship Him in the last days. Jonah's ministry sparks revival among the nations, and Micah reminds Israel that God will redeem them through the Son of David. Nahum highlights how God's vengeance and compassion cannot be separated, which allows Habakkuk and Joel to find hope in the midst of God's pending judgment upon all nations on the day of the LORD. These prophets understand that God is continuing His mission to bless humanity despite humanity's persistent idolatry and sin. He will restore the fortunes of His people.

THE TWELVE MINOR PROPHETS, PART 3

Haggai, Zechariah, and Malachi

"Behold, I will send my messenger, and he shall prepare the way before me."
—Malachi 3:1

The ending of the Twelve covers the time when some of those exiled from Judah return from Babylon to the land of Canaan. Haggai emphasizes the people's unwillingness to build a new temple for God, but God calls them to rebuild His temple so that they may, through their work, hope in what God Himself will build in the last days. Zechariah offers a series of visions that calls God's people to understand their coming judgment and the hope of a future return to God. Malachi answers the complaints of God's people with a reminder that God's affection for Israel is bound up in them remembering the Torah. Before the coming of the day of the LORD, His people wait for God's messenger to pave the way for the promised Son of David.

HAGGAI

The prophet Haggai calls Zerubbabel, Judah's governor (who is from David's family), and Joshua, the High Priest, to lead God's people to rebuild the temple. The people contend that it is not yet time to rebuild God's house, but these leaders direct the people to rebuild it.

Their well-intentioned work cannot, however, truly rebuild what Solomon built. Their new temple seems to be less glorious than the original, but God promises that this new house will indeed be greater than the old one. God strengthens them by setting His Spirit among them. God, through Haggai, promises that God will shake the whole creation in His last judgment so that all nations may come to enjoy God at God's house amid a battle of nations. However, these people are by nature unclean. They cannot build a house to hold God any more than Solomon could. Nonetheless, their work matters to God because it previews God's last work by the Son of David, when He will dwell with His people in His house.

ZECHARIAH

Zechariah offers a series of visions that bring God's people hope as they wait for the last days. While the prior generations of Israelites waited to repent until *after* God's wrath, Zechariah calls God's people to repent now. In these visions, God unveils a future time of judgment for the nations and a renewal of God's city. Various people from many different nations will become God's people.

Zechariah then receives a vision of Joshua, the High Priest, with his priestly brothers standing before God in the heavens. Although they are due death in God's presence, they find life. God declares their work meaningful and a symbol of the greater priesthood of the Son of David.

The next visions explicate the coming judgment and God's Spirit leading His anointed ones. God will remove the wickedness of human kingdoms, and His wrath will eventually be satisfied. Life will come after judgment for God's people.

Zechariah declares that the work of building God's house will be done by the Son of David, who will be a king and a priest. Those from God's people and the nations who have been returned from exile will build this house with Him. However, those who have already returned from Babylon have no heart to love God. They have returned to their homeland but not to God. Their return merely *previews* the great return to God, which will come in the last days. In the last days, the nations will walk alongside God's people with joyous excitement to return to God.

Zechariah then turns to proclaim to the nations that the Son of David is coming to judge them. The Son of David will be a king who will humbly bring God's salvation to Jerusalem. God's people will be blessed in His presence, and a great battle of nations will be answered by God's triumph and by pouring out His Spirit on His people. Then, the Son of David will be the last king. All of God's people will continually worship Him in a great Feast of Booths, a feast from the Torah about God dwelling with people in His tent, the tabernacle, which will mark His people as Holy in His presence. Idolatry and idolaters, even Canaanites, will be gone on this last day.

MALACHI

Malachi confronts God's people, who complain as their fathers did. God loves His people by providing them with His presence. In this way, He hates those who are far from Him. God's coming judgment, however, will extend God's kingdom beyond His loved people to include those who face His wrath. Thus far, God's priests and people have abused the privilege of life with God. They need, instead, to embrace and share the right knowledge of God and to love others, especially their own wives.

After God's people protest that God's judgment is absent or delayed, He answers with a reminder of His mercy and judgment at Mount Sinai. God's messenger will prepare the way for God suddenly coming to His temple. Their delight in the arrival of the Messenger of the Covenant will turn to fear because no human may stand in His presence. Israel needs to repent and obey God's words before He comes.

God's Messenger

Malachi promises that God's lesser messenger (a prophet who will come before the Messiah) will prepare the way for God's final Messenger, God Himself. Just as many prophets declared God's message as His messengers throughout the Old Testament, so this pattern will continue until the promised person comes, the Prophet Like Moses and the Son of David, in the last days. Malachi finds these ideas in Exodus after the sin of the golden calf. So that idolatrous Israel may live and not be destroyed for their idolatry by God's complete presence, God promises in Exo 32:32–33:3 to send lesser messengers and to delay sending His complete presence when the Final Messenger will end idolatry.

Some fear God and turn away from their sins. God writes their names in His book. The day of the LORD approaches, and those who fear God will rejoice on that day. God's people should wait for it by remembering the Torah. God will send a lesser messenger like Elijah, who himself was a prophet like Moses but not the Prophet Like Moses, before the day of the LORD. The lesser messenger and the Final Messenger will renew the family of God's people and will protect them all when God's Kingdom comes to end all idolatry on the day of the LORD.

KEY TAKEAWAYS

Haggai calls God's people to build His temple while waiting for the Son of David, which highlights how God's past with Israel previews humanity's future with God. Zechariah offers a series of prophetic night visions that call God's people to understand His future judgment and relish the enduring hope of a future return to God by the Son of David. Malachi answers the complaints of God's people with a reminder that God's affection for Israel is dependent upon them remembering the Torah as they wait for God's messenger to pave the way for the promised Son of David before the coming of the day of the LORD.

THE WRITINGS, AN OVERVIEW

A Focus on Divine Wisdom

> "Blessed are all they that put their trust in him."
> —Psalm 2:12

This section gives a brief overview of the third part of the Old Testament, the Writings. Psalms begins the first half of the Writings with a focus on the Son of David as God's king, who meditates upon the Torah day and night. It leads into a series of books primarily focused on divine wisdom: Job, Proverbs, Ruth, Song of Songs, Ecclesiastes, and Lamentations. The second half of the Writings begins with Esther and Daniel, which are surprising narratives of God's work among His exiled people. It continues with narratives of God's people's return to the land of Canaan in Ezra and Nehemiah. The last book of the Writings and the Old Testament is 1 and 2 Chronicles. Beginning with Adam, 1 and 2 Chronicles hurries through Israel's history to slow down when it arrives at David and his sons who rule after him so that we may understand the hope of the Son of David.

THE WRITINGS AS A BOOK

Unlike our English order of the Old Testament, the Hebrew orders follow the Torah and the Prophets with the Writings. The various Hebrew orders of the Writings reflect multiple ways that these books were read together. The order *Bible 101* follows is seen in one of the most important manuscript families, but it is not the only order. The most important difference in these orders is how the Writings ends, especially since it is also the ending for the whole Old Testament.

In some orders, the Writings ends with Ezra and Nehemiah, which sets a rather pessimistic tone where the reader finds hope in a tradition ill-equipped to change human hearts. However, the order used in Bible 101 follows Ezra and Nehemiah with 1 and 2 Chronicles. While the events described in 1 and 2 Chronicles chronologically precede the events of Ezra and Nehemiah, Chronicles works well as a follow-up to them because of how it ends. Ezra begins with a gentile king named Cyrus giving a decree to build a house for God in Jerusalem, and Chronicles ends with a shortened form of this same decree. Ezra and Nehemiah examine what happens after the decree in the past, but Chronicles sets the last word of the Old Testament in the mouth of Cyrus the gentile king anticipating what God is doing next. Chronicles' ending reads the Old Testament as anticipating the future fulfillment of its promises in the last days.

THE BOOK OF PSALMS AND DIVINE WISDOM

The Writings begins with the book of Psalms. Psalm 1 presents a Blessed Man who meditates upon the Torah day and night who will prosper in the last judgment. Psalm 2 clarifies that this Blessed Man is the Son of David, God's King. The next 148 psalms revisit and develop Psalms 1 and 2, drawing out a poetic story of how God will redeem His people through the life, death, and resurrection of the Son of David.

Job is a man blessed by God. He has walked in divine wisdom, and he has been very successful. However, through no fault of his own, he loses everything but his wife and life. His calamity leads Job to lament the day of his birth and to a contentious discussion with three of his friends about God and suffering, urging readers to hold on to the surpassing value of God's wisdom. Proverbs follows Job with its own examination of divine wisdom through the prism of Solomon. Solomon's wisdom covers every area of life, but the book looks for divine wisdom in knowing the name of God and His Son. The book of Ruth, then, shows a Moabite woman who becomes a wise, virtuous woman by binding her life to God's promise to Abraham. Song of Solomon (Song of Songs) and Ecclesiastes examine Solomon's life and the search for divine wisdom in an erotic love poem and in a perplexing sermon. Finally, Lamentations reflects poetically on Jerusalem's destruction and the need to wait for God's mercies.

Divine Wisdom

Divine Wisdom surpasses human wisdom because of how things end: man's death in God's presence. True wisdom, therefore, pulls together eschatology, the study of how things end, and ethics, how one should live. The last day, the day of the LORD, unveils God's wisdom perfectly everywhere.

THE NARRATIVES OF EXILE AND RETURN

Esther takes the reader to God's exiled people under a Persian king. The book does not mention God directly, but it offers the reader hope in God's future saving hand by revisiting the Torah. Both Esther and her adoptive father, Mordecai, will remind the reader of Joseph. In the same way that God was at work in the Torah to take care of

Joseph in exile so now God continues to work to redeem and sustain His people. Daniel also shows God's people in exile, setting Daniel as someone else who looks like Joseph. The book calls readers to be faithful through the last days by reading and heeding the Torah.

Ezra and Nehemiah present narratives of God's people's return to Judah and Jerusalem. They rebuild the temple and the walls of the city, but neither Ezra nor Nehemiah can turn the people's hearts to love God completely. Finally, 1 and 2 Chronicles revisits the whole Old Testament and draws a spotlight on the promise found in 2 Samuel 7. After examining all the rulers of Judah in search of the Son of David, a gentile king named Cyrus finishes the book. He calls for and anticipates the Son of David building God's house.

KEY TAKEAWAYS

Psalms begins the first half of the Writings with a focus on the Son of David as God's King. It leads into a series of books primarily focused on divine wisdom: Job, Proverbs, Ruth, Song of Songs, Ecclesiastes, and Lamentations. The second half of the Writings begins with Esther and Daniel, shocking narratives of God's work among His exiled people. It continues with stories of God's people's return to the land in Ezra and Nehemiah. 1 and 2 Chronicles ends the Writings by beginning with Adam and walking through Israel's history to offer future hope in the Son of David.

PSALMS

Poems for the Son of David

"The heavens declare the glory of God."
—Psalm 19:1

Psalms contains one hundred fifty poems that form one book subdivided into five books. Its many poems are attributed to multiple authors, who are listed in brief openings to many psalms. These "superscriptions" are brief openings to the poems that occasionally suggest a context from earlier in the Old Testament and offer a road map to which psalms should be read together. From its beginning to its end, Psalms forms a symphonic story that examines David's life as a preview of the Son of David and as an example of someone trusting and seeking refuge in the Son of David.

PSALMS 1–2: THE OVERTURE

Psalm 1 introduces the reader to the Blessed Man, who meditates upon the Torah day and night. He avoids the wicked ones' counsel, the sinners' path, and the scoffers' throne because He delights in the Torah. This man will prosper and arise in the last judgment, but the wicked ones and sinners will perish and not arise in the congregation of the righteous ones.

Psalm 2 answers Psalm 1's promise of the wicked perishing with the reality that gentile kings rebel against God. From His heavenly throne, God promises His wrath through His anointed King, the Son of David. God calls this King "His Son" and promises to give Him the creation as His inheritance. Though He will shatter those who oppose

Him, God warns these gentile kings to repent before the Son of David because everyone who seeks refuge in Him will be blessed with Him.

Hebrew Poetry

The book of Psalms is Hebrew poetry. Like English poetry, it stresses metaphorical and figurative language to communicate. Unlike English poetry, it emphasizes writing with brevity that creates questions for the reader and repetitions that answer those questions and pull different poetic lines together.

PSALMS 3–41: BOOK 1

Psalms 3–18 express David's heart during many painful moments. Although his own son Absalom and many others betray David, God's saving hand preserves him through struggles. He seeks refuge in God, desiring to live with Him on His holy hill.

Psalms 19–25 show David meditating on the Torah and declaring that God saves His Anointed, the Son of David. Though He will face death, the Son of David will triumph over it, rule all kingdoms, and declare who God is and teach His work to a people yet to be born. In Psalms 26–41, David proves desperate for God's saving hand. Even when his close friend betrays him, his victory will be sitting in God's presence forever.

PSALMS 42–72: BOOK 2

In Psalms 42–49, the sons of Korah beg for God's deliverance because He is their refuge and strength in the day of trouble. After one psalm from Asaph, who is a faithful musician, Psalms 51–65 highlight David's repentance after his adultery with Bathsheba (discussed in 2 Samuel). After two anonymous psalms, David asks God to scatter and conquer his enemies in Psalms 68–72. Even David's failed son Solomon knows that all kings and nations will bow down to the Son of David.

PSALMS 73–89: BOOK 3

In Psalms 73–83, Asaph remembers the wicked ones' terrible final fate before God. God's patience in judging Israel and the nations leaves His people with questions of when His wrath will end. They need His deliverance. The sons of Korah proclaim in Psalms 84–85 that salvation in God is near to those who fear Him, but David prays in Psalm 86, asking for God's help and deliverance from death. In Psalms 87–88, the sons of Korah end their poems with the pressing need for God to no longer hide His face, which leads Psalm 89 (at the end of Book 3) to ask how long God's people will wait for the Son of David.

PSALMS 90–106: BOOK 4

Book 4 answers this question by meditating on the Torah, beginning with Moses' Psalm 90. Waiting for the Son of David will take a very long time, but Psalms 90–100 offer hope that God will confirm the work of His hands as His King and Kingdom approach. Psalms 101 and 103 from David surround the psalm of an afflicted man in Psalm 102. His days are short and his body is weakened, yet the work of God's hands will sustain him. The final psalms of Book 4 revisit the Torah, asking God to return His people from exile. The wait for the Son of David will be a long time, but God will still be present while His people wait.

PSALMS 107-150: BOOK 5

Psalm 107 answers Book 4's meditating on the Torah with thankfulness to God for how He saves. In Psalms 108-110, David wrestles with his enemies, but he also defines the Son of David as God's priestly King. The following psalms praise God for His work through this King, the Son of God. In Psalm 119, the psalmist meditates upon the Torah as the way to live life with God. God's word communicates His presence with His people. This delight in the Torah leads to Psalms 120-134, the songs of ascents, that celebrate God's good work in the Son of David. David speaks one last time in Psalms 138-145. While he still cries out to God for help with problem after problem, he also delights in God's salvation. God subdues David's own people under him, and David sings of God saving gentile kings. Finally, Psalms 146-150 celebrate God's salvation by praising Him.

KEY TAKEAWAYS

The Psalms move quickly through David's life to his hope in the Son of David. Books 1 and 2 follow David's life as a picture of the Son of David's life and the life of someone seeking refuge in Him. Book 3 considers hope after David's time and leads to the question of how long God's people will wait for the Son of David. Book 4 answers that question by meditating on the Torah and learning that it will be a long wait, but God will be present by His word while His people wait. Book 5 worships and praises God's saving hand.

JOB

Holding On to Divine Wisdom

> "Behold, the fear of the Lord, that is wisdom;
> and to depart from evil is understanding."
> —Job 28:28

The wealthy Job lives uprightly for God, but unbearable loss shatters his life. While the book's message is not about his suffering, his agony is the setting to teach the reader to cling to divine wisdom. Even though all people suffer, we rarely know why. In the midst of such common ignorance, this book teaches us not to presume knowledge that we cannot know. We should instead focus on what we do know: God's good and powerful presence in our lives through His word.

Three of Job's "friends" erroneously determine that sin must be the cause of his suffering. Their analysis is wrong and spurs Job to sin in response to them. A fourth man, Elihu, offers his own counsel: Perhaps God is disciplining Job. The author prefers this answer that paves the way for God Himself answering Job with questions that no man can answer. In the end, Job repents of his words that answered his misguided friends. God restores Job's fortunes and overturns the captivity of his plagued life.

JOB 1–2: THE NARRATIVE PROLOGUE

Job lives a blameless and upright life with great riches and ten children. He turns away from evil and fears God. Every day, he continually intercedes as a priest for his family. From the heavens,

God praises Job's conduct and life, but Satan contends that if God removes Job's wealth, he will curse God because Job surely loves God's blessings rather than God Himself. God then permits Satan to harm Job's possessions and children, but not Job himself. In one day, Job loses his wealth and all ten of his children. He tears his clothes in grief but blesses God. Job does not sin or blame God.

From the heavens, God again proclaims Job's integrity, but Satan contends that Job will curse God if he harms his body. He permits Satan to afflict Job's body but not to take his life. Satan covers Job's body with painful sores, and his wife counsels him to curse God. Job rejects her words. He must accept adversity from God, not just the good. Job does not sin with his lips. Three of his friends, Eliphaz, Bildad, and Zophar, come to comfort Job. They tear their clothes and remain silent with him for seven days.

JOB 3–14: CYCLE 1 OF THE CONVERSATION BETWEEN JOB AND HIS FRIENDS

Job laments his birth and does not understand why God brought him such inexplicable suffering. He wants to know why, but there is no answer. His friends then provide their own words, which rebuke Job wrongly. They presume knowledge and charge Job with sinning when the author has shown that his suffering is not from sin. They do not know what the author showed the reader about God's conversations in heaven. As such, Eliphaz fears that Job sins because, in his mind, Job's words forget that God does not cause the innocent to perish. He counsels him to repent of sin and enjoy God's blessing.

Job despairs over this guidance—he does not know of any sin from which to repent. Then Bildad makes fundamentally the same case. Job needs to repent because God is just. Job knows that God is good, but he does not know why he suffers. Zophar, too, calls for Job to repent of his hidden sin, but Job repeats his desire to hear from God.

JOB 15–21: CYCLE 2 OF THE CONVERSATION BETWEEN JOB AND HIS FRIENDS

Eliphaz and then Bildad push back against Job. They remind him that the wicked suffer. These words torment Job, who finds hatred from God and rejection by men, yet he knows that his redeemer lives. Critiquing Job again, Zophar says that the wicked person's success is short-lived because God will give him his appropriate ending. Job remains perplexed at this accusation. Job asks whether man can understand God's judgment when He treats everyone the same.

JOB 22–31: CYCLE 3 OF THE CONVERSATION BETWEEN JOB AND HIS FRIENDS

Eliphaz charges Job with great wickedness, and Bildad argues no man can be right in God's sight. Job's complaints grow, and his desire to hear from God multiplies. He claims innocence—he keeps God's path and treasures His words more than his own food! God is exceedingly greater than all, and He will judge all wickedness. Man will search for all sorts of treasure throughout the world, but no man can find wisdom in material creation alone. Job longs for divine wisdom, and only God can provide it. Man may look for it, but it is found only through fearing God and turning from evil. Job maintains his innocence and still longs to hear from God.

JOB 32–37: ELIHU'S ANSWER TO JOB

Suddenly, a younger friend, Elihu, speaks up. The question is not Job's righteousness or God's. Job's suffering is borne of God's discipline. He wants Job to open his ears to instruction. God is the teacher whose work is not in the storm, its rolling thunder and lightning. His work is in His voice.

Who Is Elihu?

Elihu is Job's friend who waits to speak because he is young. His anger burns against Job for justifying himself before God when Job answered the three friends, so he advises Job that God is disciplining him with a message that prepares for God's speeches. His name means "He is my God."

JOB 38–41: GOD ANSWERS JOB

God answers Job in a storm by turning the tables and asking Job unanswerable questions. God says that He will await instruction from Job. These mocking words prove the foolishness of trying to instruct God. God asks where was Job when God created all things?

With each successive question, the gap between God and man increases. Job has no words in reply. He must remain silent in His presence, but God continues with more unanswerable questions. Job repents for his words in the conversation because they presumed knowledge beyond what people can know.

JOB 42: THE NARRATIVE EPILOGUE

God rebukes Eliphaz and his two friends because they did not speak rightly of God, even though Job did through his repentance. God asks them to have Job sacrifice several animals on their behalf. Eliphaz, Bildad, and Zophar do as God asks, and God accepts Job.

God restores Job's fortunes and overturns the captivity of his plagued life, doubling all of his wealth and his children. His three daughters are fairer than any others and receive an inheritance among their brothers.

KEY TAKEAWAYS

In the same way that most people do not know why they suffer, Job finds himself at a loss to know why he suffers. People cannot know why God does all things. They know only in part, and rarely do they know why God acts in particular situations. Instead, people must hang on to divine wisdom when they find no answer to why they hurt. They need to admit that human knowledge is limited, but God's knowledge is not. In the end, people must trust God, repent of known sin, and wait for Him to restore fortunes and overturn captivity, as He did for Job.

PROVERBS

The Son of David's Wisdom

> "The fear of the LORD is the beginning of knowledge:
> but fools despise wisdom and instruction."
> —Proverbs 1:7

David's son Solomon is the wisest man who ever lived, but he made himself a fool by disobeying the Torah. Proverbs examines Solomon's wisdom in light of divine wisdom. Solomon's proverbial statements examine every part of life, and they leave the reader with an extensive list of things to do, avoid, and consider. The author frames these proverbial wisdom statements about life in the world with two conversations. At the book's beginning, a father advises his son to avoid Lady Folly and to pursue Lady Wisdom. He shows wisdom being with God at creation. At its ending, another speaker finds divine wisdom in knowing the name of God and His Son.

PROVERBS 1:1–7: THE OPENING

This brief opening establishes the book's subject matter: the proverbs of Solomon. The book's design helps readers to gain God's wisdom and instruction, transforming anyone humble enough to heed its words. Wise people will gain wisdom through the good fear of God.

PROVERBS 1:8–9:18:
A FATHER COUNSELS HIS SON
AND OTHER SONS

An unnamed father repeatedly calls to his son as he shares wisdom. After advising his son to follow his parents' teachings, the father warns his son to avoid those who entice him with sin.

He also presents divine wisdom as a woman, Lady Wisdom. She shouts in the busy streets, but no one listens to her. She promises, however, that if people repent of their sin when they hear her words, they will receive her Spirit. God will let her words be known. This father promises his son that receiving his words will yield wisdom so that he will be able to identify righteousness and justice. It will also deliver him from the strange woman, the Lady Folly, whose path leads to death. He should trust in God and reject his own understandings when they conflict with God's understanding and even when he may face God's discipline. God's wisdom is a tree of life that will protect and provide for him as he tries to apply God's principles.

Lady Wisdom

Throughout the Writings, the authors portray wisdom as a woman, Lady Wisdom, because they are commenting on Eve's desire to be wise in the garden and her foolish abandonment of God's word. Unlike Eve, however, Lady Wisdom clings to and proclaims God's word and provides God's Spirit.

The father also addresses multiple other sons with this same wisdom so that all of them may prosper from his words. These other sons must follow the same counsel as the one son: Avoid the adulteress woman whose flattery and seduction lead to death. It is very common for a young man to see Lady Folly lurking at every corner. She will approach him openly and promise him his desires with no consequences. In the end, however, he has been trapped by his desires. All his sons must know that Lady Folly leads to death.

Wisdom, however, calls out to these young men if they will hear it. Wisdom speaks of truth and nobility and dwells with prudence. Lady Wisdom was with God at creation in the beginning, so everything reflects her voice. Lady Wisdom has built her house for those who will seek her. Fools will seek Lady Folly, and they will learn the hard way that such stolen delights, being driven by desires contrary to God's desires, lead to death.

PROVERBS 10:1–24:24: SOLOMON'S PROVERBS WITH THE SAYINGS OF THE WISE

The proverbial statements of Solomon begin with a son's impact upon his parents and then pivot line by line to discuss how wisdom can be applied to every area of life. These statements have discernible patterns when read carefully. Every area of life requires God's wisdom, and every proverb has a particular context. These proverbial statements, usually grouped in two connected lines, also leave the reader with a sense of how success lies in one area and failure in another. Across these wisdom statements, honest readers cannot claim to be wise on their own. As proverbs continue line after line, the "sayings of the wise" supplement Solomon's proverbs because the book's wisdom surpasses Solomon's wisdom.

PROVERBS 25:1–29:27: MORE OF SOLOMON'S PROVERBS

Solomon's next group of proverbial statements is developed and joined together during the days of Hezekiah. As with the rest of the book, these proverbial statements do not contradict each other, but they require the reader to learn wisdom to discern which proverbial statement to apply. For example, should someone answer a fool when he speaks up? On one hand, to answer a fool may render one like the fool. On the other hand, to *not* answer a fool may be harmful to the fool. We need wisdom to know which wisdom proverb to heed.

PROVERBS 30:1–33: AGUR'S QUESTIONS AND ANSWERS

With Solomon's words completed, an unknown man named Agur declares that he lacks understanding. He longs for the knowledge of God. Wisdom comes down to two questions about God: "What is his name, and what is his son's name?" (Pro 30:4). Agur repeats and adds to Moses' question at the burning bush: "What is His name?" Agur wants to find God's wisdom lived out in His Son, a person who actually embodies God's wisdom. These insights lead Agur to examine God's word.

PROVERBS 31:1–31: LEMUEL'S WORDS AND THE VIRTUOUS WOMAN

King Lemuel, who, like Agur, is unknown, applies his mother's wisdom to ruling well as a king. Whereas Solomon stumbled with his many wives and abandoned wisdom, Lemuel's mother counsels Lemuel to direct his passions with women, drink, and power to do what is good. The book ends with a search for a wise woman: "Who can find a virtuous woman?" (Pro 31:10). This question accomplishes at least two things:

1. It compels young men to search for a woman who fears God.
2. It implies that God can find such a woman and also prepare such a woman for His Son, the person Agur seeks.

This woman's description also reflects Lady Wisdom. Those who fear God rightly will receive His wisdom and become His bride.

KEY TAKEAWAYS

The book of Proverbs examines Solomon's proverbial wisdom in search of divine wisdom that is greater than Solomon's wisdom. The reader must chase after Lady Wisdom and know the name of God and His son, a person who walks in this wisdom perfectly. Divine wisdom is needed to know which Solomonic proverb to apply and where to find hope when the reader has not lived out these proverbs. These proverbs teach people where they lack wisdom and how far they are from living God's perfect will so that they can seek after the person who does: God's son.

RUTH AND SONG OF SOLOMON (OR SONG OF SONGS)

A Virtuous Woman and Waiting for the Son of David

"My beloved is mine, and I am his."
—Song of Solomon 2:16

As Proverbs ends with a search for a virtuous woman, the book of Ruth presents the Moabite Ruth as such a virtuous woman because she binds herself to Israel's God. She and her Israelite mother-in-law return to Canaan after their husbands die. How will God care for these women and protect the names of their dead Israelite husbands? He does so through a man who obeys the Torah, Boaz. Boaz and Ruth marry and have a son, whose family leads to David. Song of Solomon (or Song of Songs) returns to the question of Solomon through an erotic love poem of a man and woman pursuing each other. The book's images lead to many different interpretations, but it echoes key moments from the Torah and Proverbs to guide readers to patiently and passionately wait for the Son of David.

RUTH'S STORY

During the days of a famine, when Israel's judges rule the land, an Israelite leads his wife, Naomi, and their two sons to Moab. His sons marry two Moabite women there, Orpah and Ruth. When all three men die, Naomi urges Orpah and Ruth to return to their fathers' houses because she cannot provide sons to care for them. Orpah complies, but Ruth clings to Naomi and promises to follow her God. Naomi and Ruth return to Canaan, but Naomi becomes bitter and sees God as afflicting her.

Why Is Ruth after Judges in English Bibles?

English Bibles set Ruth after Judges because the book's events take place at the same time as Judges. However, Ruth was originally a part of the Writings, providing commentary on how to understand the virtuous woman of Proverbs 31.

To feed Naomi and herself, Ruth finds the field of a man named Boaz and gathers the leftover crops not picked up by the hired workers. Boaz sees her labor and knows that she is taking care of Naomi. Heeding the Torah's command to protect the foreigner, he offers to protect her by having her gather in his field with his maidens. Boaz asks for God's favor on her work since she is seeking refuge under His wings.

Ruth excitedly reports her good favor to Naomi. Naomi alerts Ruth that Boaz is part of their extended family, a close relative; Ruth must heed his word. Because the Torah commands God's men to care for the widow of a brother, Naomi urges Ruth to lie down at his feet. When he sees her at the foot of his bed, Boaz delights that she chose him. He will follow her request to care for her because everyone knows her to be a virtuous woman. A man who is an even closer relative, however, has the right to marry Ruth.

Boaz approaches the gates of the city of Bethlehem and its elders to find the closer relative and to see if the closer relative wants to marry Ruth. If this closer relative marries Ruth, his firstborn and inheritance will be named after Ruth's deceased husband. The closer relative declines. Before the elders and all the people of the city, Boaz declares he will marry Ruth and care for her and Naomi. Boaz marries Ruth, and they have a son, whom Naomi nurses. This son becomes the father of Jesse, who is the father of David.

THE SONG OF SOLOMON
(OR SONG OF SONGS)

In the Song of Solomon, Solomon's affection for his beloved and her affection for him yield an erotic poem of their mutual sexual passion. Solomon's own story, of course, creates tension with this poem. After all, Solomon married hundreds of women and also had hundreds of concubines. Both the synagogue and the church have wrestled with how to understand this book. Most read the Song as an allegory of either God's love for Israel or Christ's love for the church. Others read the poem as a meaningful depiction of sex within marriage. A few read it as a three-part love story where Solomon is not the man desiring love, but the obstacle to the man's and woman's desires.

Amid these compelling views, one more view remains that brings together insights from the allegorical and literal approaches. Because the book's poetry echoes moments from the Torah and Proverbs, these refrains from other parts of the Old Testament allow the poem to compare the lovers' mutual passions to how the Son of David will pursue Lady Wisdom. The author links the couple's desires to Adam and Eve's failures in the garden, Mount Sinai, Solomon's own failures, and Proverbs' discussion of God's teaching on the heart to call for the Son of David to do what Solomon fails to do.

The Erotic Poem

The poem itself does not describe who is speaking, although most translations define each speaker. When the speaker proclaims the beauty of female body parts, it is the man speaking. When the glory of male body parts is discussed, the woman speaks. Their poem also includes two "choruses," the daughters of Jerusalem and the woman's brothers.

The poem begins with their longings for each other. She repeatedly calls for his left hand to be under her head and his right hand to embrace her in a vivid pleading for consummation. She also repeatedly warns the daughters of Jerusalem not to arouse such love until the right time.

The lovers are separated from each other throughout the poem, so she desires that they could be like a brother and sister, who could be close to each other while they wait. At the book's ending, she is still waiting for him and sees him as the one who will overturn Eve's fall in the garden because his love will be a seal over his heart and will overcome death. The author sets his hope not on Solomon but on the Son of David, who will bring consummation in God's garden. She calls out for him to hurry.

KEY TAKEAWAYS

Ruth lives as a virtuous woman because she binds herself to Israel's God. God cares for her and her mother-in-law, preserving the names of their deceased husbands through marrying a man, Boaz, who continually obeys the Torah. Their son's family leads to David. Song of Solomon (Song of Songs) then considers Solomon, a son of David, through an erotic love poem. The book directs readers to hear its echoes of the Torah and Proverbs as a guide in how to read the poem well. The lovers' mutual affection encourages us to wait for the Son of David, whose love for Lady Wisdom will bring God's people to live with God.

ECCLESIASTES AND LAMENTATIONS

Finding Life's Meaning in a Broken World

"Fear God, and keep his commandments: for this is the whole duty of man."
—Ecclesiastes 12:13

In Ecclesiastes, Solomon preaches about life and examines its apparent meaninglessness. He pursues purpose and life under the shadow of humankind's mortality and his own powerlessness to change himself or the world. The author frames the sermon with an introduction and conclusion that tell the reader how to handle its most difficult passages. Most importantly, the book's conclusion sees God's wisdom as fearing God and obeying His commandments because God is the last judge. Lamentations grieves over Jerusalem's destruction after the Babylonians obliterate the city. It laments that the city where God set His name looks like a destitute widow. The God who judges Jerusalem is also the God whose mercy offers hope in the end.

ECCLESIASTES

In this book, Solomon preaches a sermon that begins with a troubling insight into life in the fallen world: "vanity of vanities; all is vanity" (Ecc 1:2). Is life a vain pursuit when death ends all things? This term for "vanity" is the same word as Abel's name in Genesis. His brother Cain murdered him after Abel lived a righteous life with God before his death. The sermon considers the implications of Abel's fate and wonders if doing what is right and good really matters when death awaits all humankind.

The sermon looks for the profit people gain from their work and life under the sun. Their daily rhythms often set their work as futile, a clasping for the wind that never changes anything.

The preacher, Solomon, seeks to find life, enjoyment, and purpose in chasing after wisdom, pleasure, riches, and work—only to discover that his death renders nothing he does as permanent. Nonetheless, he examines all of life and sees that there is a time and a season for every emotion and action, but God has set man's heart to not be satisfied with what he sees, knows, and hears. Instead, God sets a desire for eternity in each man's heart that the material world cannot fill.

A Time for Everything

The preacher, Solomon, contends that there is a time for everything because life is so broad. One proverb does not apply to every situation. Instead, true wisdom connects man's life to God's eternal story to bring meaning, purpose, and love to our good and bad days.

The preacher sees the oppression in the world and finds the dead have it better than the living in many ways. In this life, he reminds us to keep our promises to God and to fear Him because even great riches cannot deliver humans from death. Wisdom comes from fearing God, and wisdom proves much better than folly. God makes people upright, but all people seek after idols in the creation rather than the Creator. The miracle is that God intervenes to change us and our desires slowly over time by grace. Time will overtake even the strongest, the fastest, and the wisest of people, and no person controls the results of a contest or how things end. The day after a man dies, his loved ones will mourn for a moment. The world, however, will go on without him, as if he has never been. "Then shall the dust return to the earth as it was: and the spirit shall return unto God who gave it" (Ecc 12:7). As he began the sermon, he concludes, "All is vanity" (Ecc 12:8).

The author affirms the wisdom of Solomon and warns against endless devotion to books. The sermon closes with a simple command because God will bring every act of good or evil to judgment: "Fear God, and keep his commandments: for this is the whole duty of man" (Ecc 12:13).

LAMENTATIONS

Lamentations begins with a question, "How?" The city of Jerusalem where God's name dwells sits alone and as desolate as a widow with little visible hope. The author wants to know not only how this happened but also how the city might be restored. This tragic poem of the aftermath of Jerusalem's destruction from Babylon is shaped in its first four chapters as a series of acrostic lines that follow the Hebrew alphabet one letter at a time.

At this time, the adversaries of God's people prosper. God Himself has brought grief upon His people because of their many sins. Jerusalem's strength is gone, and God seems like an enemy to His own people. They no longer teach the Torah, prophets no longer have visions from God, and the elders sit silently with dust on their heads. God acts according to His purposes as His word decrees, so the author asks God to remember his affliction. The book reads, "This I recall to my mind, therefore have I hope. It is of the LORD'S mercies that we are not consumed, because his compassions fail not. They are new every morning: great is thy faithfulness" (Lam 3:21–23).

The destruction of Jerusalem ushers in a new season of waiting for God's mercies to be made visible. God is good to those who wait for Him because God will not reject forever. Trusting God in this world requires a future hope because God scatters His people in exile among all the nations. God promises a day when punishment and discipline will end for His people. Yet the same punishment will spread to all nations. The final plea of the book calls out for God to renew and make visible His affection for His people. May God not forget them, and may He restore them to live life with Him.

KEY TAKEAWAYS

These two books teach readers of God's presence in the fallen and broken world. As man was exiled from God because of Adam's sin in Genesis, so God's people find themselves struggling to live life with God. They, too, find exile. Ecclesiastes helps us understand how we should live when life itself seems broken beyond our repair. Like Abel in Genesis who trusted God and still found death, we must trust God and fear His commandments because only God's word can bring hope in life and death. He is the judge of all of humanity's actions. Such despair multiplies in Lamentations as the city where God's name has been established lies in ruin. Its destruction, however, reminds people that their hope is in God, whose mercy is new each day. We must wait for the house and city that the Son of David will build.

ESTHER

God's Surprising Presence in Exile

> "And the king took off his ring, which he had taken from Haman,
> and gave it unto Mordecai."
> —Esther 8:2

During Judah's exile, a Benjamite named Mordecai and his "adopted daughter," Esther, live under Persian rule. Surprisingly, Esther finds herself elevated to queen, but the other great leader of the land is Haman, a sworn enemy of the Jewish people. He sets out to destroy God's people because of Mordecai and his refusal to bow down to him. Haman persuades the king to set a day when all Jewish people may be killed. When hope seems lost, Esther heeds Mordecai's counsel and approaches the king and finds life for her and all Israel. Instead of Israel being destroyed on that day, Israel's enemies face judgment. As Haman is judged, the king exalts Mordecai into Haman's old position as second in command. Mordecai's service brings good to the whole nation.

ESTHER'S BACKGROUND FROM THE TORAH AND THE PROPHETS

The only book in the Bible that does not directly reference God is Esther, but it communicates who God is and what He is doing by alluding to the Torah. With the Torah, God's hand can be traced through the events of Esther's book. These Torah echoes begin in Genesis with Esau and Jacob:

twin brothers whose rivalry extends to their nations. Jacob becomes Israel, and Esau becomes Edom. One of Esau's grandsons becomes the nation Amalek, which fights against God's people when Israel leaves Egypt. With Moses' raised arms, God gives Israel victory. Moses writes down Amalek's last judgment and describes a constant conflict between Israel and Amalek until the end. Balaam (a gentile prophet) also proclaims the Messiah will destroy Amalek in the last days.

Years later, Saul, a Benjamite and son of Kish, serves as Israel's first king. Samuel commands him to annihilate an Amalekite town. Saul does not and keeps alive its king, Agag, and some of the choice animals for sacrifice. Samuel rebukes Saul and slays Agag, whose family survives because of Saul. At the end of Saul's life, an Amalekite falsely takes credit for killing Saul. David executes this Amalekite just after he defeats many Amalekites in a great battle. The Book of Esther portrays conflict between a descendant of Saul, Mordecai, and a descendant of Agag, Haman. God protects His people in extraordinary ways, but the author longs for the last days when He will provide complete victory.

THE BOOK OF ESTHER

Amid the grandeur of his empire, the Persian king Ahasuerus throws a half-year party that leads to his queen being cast from her throne. The king's men seek a new queen for Ahasuerus by gathering young virgins together into a harem.

A young, exiled orphan from Judah named Esther lives with her "uncle," Mordecai. He is from the family of Saul and Benjamin and advises Esther (as she is brought into the harem) to keep her Jewish identity a secret. The king tests the women and Esther becomes the queen. Only Mordecai knows she is a Jewish person.

Later, Mordecai overhears two guards plotting to murder the king. He relays the message to Esther, who in turn informs the king. The king's life is saved, and the conspirators are executed. Shortly thereafter, Mordecai refuses to bow down to the king's right-hand man, Haman, who is from the family of Esau, Amalek, and Agag. Haman's rage against Mordecai becomes a lust to kill his people. He bribes the king to enact a day of judgment for all Jewish people.

When Mordecai learns of the decree, he sends Esther a copy, wanting her to speak with the king. However, Esther cannot see the king except under the penalty of death if she approaches uninvited. Mordecai reminds her that she cannot escape the decree's judgment. If she does not act to save Israel, their deliverance will arise from another person. It may be that she is in this lofty position for the purpose of saving Israel.

Esther approaches the king, and he lets her live. She does not make her request known right away. Instead, she invites the king and Haman to a banquet. At this banquet, Esther invites the king and Haman to yet another banquet on the next day. This special treatment fills Haman with pride. Haman follows his wife's counsel to build a gallows to hang Mordecai. That night, however, the king cannot sleep. He remembers that Mordecai saved his life, and no one honored him. As Haman approaches, the king asks him how to honor a great man. Believing that the honor is for him, Haman advises the king to plan a grand procession. To Haman's dismay, the king honors Mordecai.

God's Presence in Irony

Following the startling narratives in Genesis, Esther reveals God's presence in ironic surprises that are either coincidental or intentional. By setting Esther in the Writings, the author refutes the notion of coincidence and encourages the reader that God's presence today echoes what is in the Torah.

Haman is brought to Esther's banquet. Her Jewish identity still remains a secret. At that time, she explains that Haman has set out to destroy her and all her people: She is a Jewish person. The king orders Haman hung on the gallows he designed for Mordecai. As Haman dies, Mordecai is raised into Haman's old job. However, Haman's decree leaves the fate of the Jewish people in jeopardy. The day of judgment cannot be avoided. Mordecai and the king send out a new decree transforming the day of judgment. Anyone who opposes the Jewish people may be judged on this new day. Many of the gentiles join with the Jewish people in defeating their enemies. This day becomes the feast of Purim.

Mordecai finds himself being celebrated. Saul's fallen house is redeemed by one who looks like Joseph. We must wait, however, for the Son of David—who looks like and surpasses both Mordecai and Joseph.

KEY TAKEAWAYS

Esther's book draws readers into a world governed by the nations, but God's good plans continue for His people despite those who oppose them. They are scattered among the nations, who may learn who God is by how He cares for them in the midst of conflict. In order to see what God is doing in this world, the reader must remember the Torah. The book of Esther's allusions to it show the reader that God is still working to accomplish all He promised Moses He would do to bring people from Israel and the nations to live with Him forever in the end.

DANIEL

Waiting for the Triumph of the Son of Man

> "Behold, one like the Son of man came with the clouds of heaven,
> and came to the Ancient of days."
> —Daniel 7:13

In the Book of Daniel, Nebuchadnezzar exiles Daniel and three of his friends to Babylon and trains them to serve in his kingdom. God protects these men in a series of narratives mostly written in Aramaic—the language of the nations—rather than Hebrew. Their faithfulness makes it possible for Nebuchadnezzar and other kings to hear about God. Daniel's service echoes Joseph's story from the Torah, offering hope for life in exile. The second half of the book moves from narratives to prophetic and apocalyptic visions of the future, the last days. The vision of Daniel 7 portrays the Son of Man; namely, the Son of David, receiving His everlasting kingdom. Except for Daniel 7, these visions are written in Hebrew and end with a promise that those who remain faithful will receive what God promises.

DANIEL 1: OBEYING GOD IN EXILE

As Nebuchadnezzar besieges Jerusalem, he exiles young nobles to learn the language and literature of Babylon, including Daniel, Shadrach, Meshach, and Abednego. This training also requires them to eat the king's food. However, Moses' law codes command Israel to *not* eat the king's food, so Daniel asks the guard to let them eat only water and vegetables. After a ten-day testing, the guard finds them in good shape and continues in this manner. God provides them with knowledge and wisdom and even gives Daniel the ability to understand dreams and visions. Nebuchadnezzar finds them the best wise men in his service, a role Daniel serves for many kings until Cyrus.

DANIEL 2–6: THE VISIONS AND TESTS FROM THE GENTILE KINGS

A dream startles Nebuchadnezzar that none of his wise men can interpret. Because none of them can help him, he seeks to kill them. However, God gives Daniel its interpretation. His vision was of a statue that divides from top to bottom in gold, then silver, bronze, iron, and iron mixed with clay. A stone cut without human hands strikes the statue, causing it to fall. The statue represents human kingdoms, but the stone signifies God's Kingdom, which will overcome all human kingdoms. Nebuchadnezzar praises Daniel's God.

Which Nations Does Daniel Refer To?

For millennia, interpreters have debated the specific nations that Daniel references in the book's visions. The best approaches look for the book's larger patterns and for the specific nations listed in the book itself rather than letting our historical moment define such.

Three Men Survive a Fire

Nebuchadnezzar builds a gold statue of himself and demands that everyone bow down to it under the penalty of death. Shadrach, Meshach, and Abednego refuse to bow down. God can save them, but they will not worship Nebuchadnezzar's idol whether or not God saves them. After casting them into the furnace, Nebuchadnezzar notices a fourth person who looks like a son of God walking in the fire with the three miraculously unharmed men. Nebuchadnezzar calls them out of the fire. Now he knows that their God is God.

Nebuchadnezzar As a Tree of Life

Later, Nebuchadnezzar has another vision that only Daniel can understand. Nebuchadnezzar is shown as a tree that gives life to everyone but is cut down. The dream also foreshadows how Nebuchadnezzar will begin to act like an animal. A year later, as his pride swells, he finds himself brought down, driven mad, and eating grass as an animal. Nebuchadnezzar repents and is returned to his throne.

Nebuchadnezzar's son, Belshazzar, holds a large party, but a hand without a body writes words upon a wall that no one but Daniel can interpret. He warns him that his kingdom is about to end because he is deficient as a man. His kingdom will be divided. That same night, he is slain, and Darius receives the kingdom.

Darius sets Daniel as one of his top rulers, which makes the other nobles jealous. They lure Darius into commanding all men to pray to Darius under the penalty of death. After Darius agrees, they bring charges against Daniel, who refuses to pray to anyone other than God. Darius tries to stop the death sentence, but he cannot. Darius assures Daniel as he is lowered into the lions' den that his God will save him. In the morning, Darius finds Daniel alive. They praise God.

DANIEL 7: THE SON OF MAN

Daniel receives a vision from God of four kings emerging from the sea as beasts. The fourth one has ten horns upon his head that give way to another little horn. God the Father, known as the Ancient of Days, sits upon a throne with myriads standing before Him. As the beasts and their kingdoms expire, one like the Son of Man approaches the Ancient of Days. This Son of David receives an everlasting Kingdom of all peoples. The beasts are four kingdoms, and the horn will afflict God's people continually until the very end, when the everlasting Kingdom will be given to them.

Apocalyptic Prophecy

Daniel 7–12 provides a series of apocalyptic visions with imagery that portrays complex future realities in symbolic, metaphorical, and figurative language. The best way to understand these images is by recognizing their echoes of earlier parts of the Old Testament, especially the Torah.

DANIEL 8–12: DANIEL'S OTHER VISIONS

In Daniel's next vision, the angel Gabriel explains that a ram arising out of the east and a goat arising out of the west are two colliding kingdoms: the Medes and Persians against the Greeks. Further clarifying Daniel 7, this vision shows the same horn prospering himself and destroying God's people until the little horn will be broken by God.

Later, Daniel tries to understand Jeremiah promising God's people a 70-year exile. Gabriel explains that this 70-year exile will actually be seventy sets of 7 years, or 490 years. In the 483rd year after the decree to rebuild Jerusalem, the promised Son of David will die. After that time, Daniel receives another vision with a great series of conflicts among kings in the land. It shows a time of distress unlike any other, but those who have insight from God and obey His voice will endure. As Daniel himself wonders how long this trauma will be, he is encouraged to stay faithful through difficult times so that he and those who trust God may rest in Him.

KEY TAKEAWAYS

God's Kingdom will prevail over all human kingdoms, and God's people, who have been scattered among all these kingdoms, will endure suffering while they wait for God's final triumph. In Daniel, the author encourages people to wait a long time for God's King, the Son of Man and the Son of David, by heeding what they know of God's word and waiting for God to explain the more difficult parts of God's word. They must not be dismayed at the defeats of God's people. They will not be the end of the story. Life with God Himself is the end of His people's story. God is their reward.

EZRA

Returning to the Land

> "O my God, I am ashamed and blush to lift up my face to thee,
> my God: for our iniquities are increased over our head,
> and our trespass is grown up unto the heavens."
> —Ezra 9:6

In various waves, God's people return from Babylon. The book of Ezra highlights those who came back after the Persian king Cyrus decrees the rebuilding of the temple for God. The returnees struggle to build a new temple for God under the leadership of Joshua, the priest, and Zerubbabel, the governor. God's people eventually heed God's words from the prophets Haggai and Zechariah and rebuild the temple. The scribe and priest Ezra also brings another group of people back to Jerusalem, but when Ezra arrives, the people are caught in the sin of intermarrying with the peoples of the surrounding nations. Ezra leads them in confession, repentance, and a renewal to the law codes of the Torah.

EZRA 1–2: CYRUS'S DECREE

To confirm the words of Jeremiah, which promised a return from the Babylonian exile after seventy years, God commands Cyrus, Persia's king, to issue a decree that God has appointed him to build His house in Jerusalem. Any of God's people who are willing should contribute to this project. From this pronouncement, a group of over forty-two thousand Israelites plus their servants return to Jerusalem. They are not the only group to return to the land.

EZRA 3–6: THE BUILDING OF THE TEMPLE

Joshua, the priest from the tribe of Levi, and Zerubbabel, the governor from the tribe of Judah and David's family, lead these returnees to build an altar and offer sacrifices according to the Torah, as they celebrate the Feast of Booths.

In the second year of this return from Babylon, Joshua and Zerubbabel lead the people to build the temple's foundation. At the sight of the foundation, many rejoice, but the older men who saw the grandeur of Solomon's temple weep because it is nothing compared to what Solomon had built. The sound of the weeping and rejoicing is so great that their enemies come forward and ask to join them in the building project. They contend that they worship the same God as the Jewish people, although they clearly worship a different god. Zerubbabel and Joshua reject their proposal because only God's people may build the house.

In response to this work on the temple and the elevation of new kings over Persia, these gentile leaders who offered to help now draft a letter in the language of Aramaic to King Artaxerxes that warns the new king of the temple building project and the city of Jersualem's history of rebellion. Artaxerxes orders the building project to stop. However, God raises up, or chooses and employs, the prophets Haggai and Zechariah to encourage Joshua and Zerubbabel to lead the people to finish building the temple. Again, the gentiles write a letter to another new king, Darius, and ask him to stop the building project. This time, Darius finds Cyrus's decree and confirms that the temple is to be rebuilt and that the gentiles will help pay. When the temple is completed, God's people appoint priests to serve in the temple according to Moses' Torah.

EZRA 7–8: EZRA PREPARES TO GO TO JERUSALEM

Ezra, the priest during the days of Artaxerxes, is a skilled scribe who copies the Torah. He receives permission from his king to bring a group of people with him to Jerusalem. Departing in the first month of Artaxerxes's seventh year, he arrives in the fifth month with priests, singers, Levites, gatekeeps, and temple servants. Under God's good hand, Ezra sets his heart to study, practice, and teach the Torah.

He carries with him the king's decree that provides riches for the building project and the treasury of the temple. It invites all of God's people to build the temple and establish its worship, as well as teach and implement its laws so that there will be no judgment on the kingdom. Ezra's group of returnees head out on their journey. When they camp, however, they discover that they have no Levites with them to care for the temple. So Ezra sends for Levites to join them. In the middle of their journey, they also declare a fast for protection and a safe journey because Ezra is ashamed to ask their king for his army's protection since he has said that God will provide protection. Upon their arrival, they add to the treasury, hand over the king's decree, and offer burnt offerings.

EZRA 9–10: CONFESSION AND REPENTANCE

The leaders of Israel approach Ezra with sad news. The returnees, especially the leaders of God's people, are violating the Torah and marrying the women from the surrounding nations. Upon hearing this news, Ezra tears his clothes and trembles at God's word. Later that night, he prays to God and confesses his shame at their sins. They are no different than their fathers whom God exiled, and Ezra has nothing to say except that they are all guilty of breaking God's commandments. Knowing that God is righteous and God's people are guilty, Ezra asks for mercy so that His wrath does not destroy all of them.

Interracial Marriage

The Bible does not forbid interracial marriage, as evidenced by Boaz's marriage to Ruth as well as other texts. It does, however, forbid believers from marrying unbelievers because of the impact on those persons and the next generation. This instruction passes God's word and life to future generations.

During his prayers, a large assembly of men come to Ezra and confess their sins. They agree to make a covenant with God to put away their foreign wives and abide by God's law codes for them as His people. Ezra leads many, but not all, of God's people in a great time of confession and recommitment to God.

KEY TAKEAWAYS

Those who returned to Jerusalem struggle to build a new temple for God. After God's people heed His words from the prophets Haggai and Zechariah, they rebuild the temple. The scribe and priest Ezra also brings another group of people back to Jerusalem, but he finds the men caught in the sin of intermarrying with the nations. Ezra leads them in confession, repentance, and a renewal to the law codes of the Torah.

NEHEMIAH

God's Work Amid Man's Work

"So they read in the book in the law of God distinctly,
and gave the sense, and caused them to understand the reading."
—Nehemiah 8:8

Nehemiah's book tells the story of rebuilding Jerusalem's walls. This effort offers a space and a place for God to do His work in His people through God's word. After the restoration of the walls, Ezra reads the Torah to all the people so that God may draw them to repentance and renewal. Afterward, they make a covenant before God to follow Him fully. However, the renewal fades over time. They are like their fathers, so the people and Nehemiah find themselves waiting on God to remember His promise to Abraham.

NEHEMIAH 1–2: NEHEMIAH RETURNS TO JERUSALEM AFTER BEING SCATTERED TO BABYLON

Nehemiah serves the Persian king Artaxerxes and hears that God's people are not doing well in Jerusalem. They are distressed, and the city walls are broken down. Nehemiah prays. He confesses God's people's sins and asks God to remember His promise in Deuteronomy

30 of a great return to God. He will restore the fortunes of His people and overturn their captivity.

The king wonders why Nehemiah looks so sad. His sadness stems from Jerusalem's deplorable state. Nehemiah asks to go to Jerusalem to rebuild it, and the king grants his request. When he arrives, he privately investigates the wall's beleaguered condition. Nehemiah then approaches Jerusalem's leaders, and they agree to build. However, the leaders of the peoples beyond the river, Sanballat and Tobiah, mock and oppose their efforts. Nehemiah promises God will give His people success.

NEHEMIAH 3–6: JERUSALEM'S WALLS ARE REBUILT

Nehemiah divides the labor into different families working on separate sections of the wall. As Sanballat and Tobiah continue mocking the wall's meager state, Nehemiah prays and asks God to judge them. The work continues, with the wall reaching half its height, despite escalating hostilities. After prayer, Nehemiah provides armed guards to protect them while they labor. To be ready for the threat of attack, the workers carry weapons along with their tools. He encourages them to trust God because He is fighting for them.

Unfortunately, the common workers have abandoned their normal jobs and incomes to build. They borrow money from their wealthier brothers to stay alive. Against the Torah's law codes, the wealthier Jewish people charge them usury, or interest, so Nehemiah condemns this practice. In response, they commit to not charge usury. Additionally, Sanballat and Tobiah repeatedly seek meetings with Nehemiah to distract him, but he declines their invitations. They also use one of the Jerusalemites to persuade Nehemiah that he must hide in the temple and stop the work because of a plot to murder him. Nehemiah discerns that this warning is a ruse and maintains his work for God. After fifty-two days, they complete the walls.

Why Does the Torah Forbid Usury?

In Deuteronomy 23, the Torah commands an Israelite to not charge his brother usury, which are fees similar to interest. Usury, however, may be charged against a foreigner, a non-brother. God's people are to live as brothers so that God may bless their work.

NEHEMIAH 7–8: EZRA LEADS THE TEACHING OF GOD'S WORD

A large group of exiles (also described in Ezra 2) returns to Jerusalem. Ezra the scribe and priest leads the people to gather in Jerusalem for Torah reading. Being surrounded by men who translate the Hebrew into the people's Aramaic language, Ezra leads them to stand for the Torah reading and teaching. Nehemiah declares that the day is holy, but the Torah makes clear that the people are sinning greatly. Weeping and grieving overwhelm the call to celebrate God's work.

On the second day of reading, they discern that they are not heeding the Torah's command to live in tents as part of the Feast of Booths, which is one of the yearly feasts commanded in the Torah. The people make temporary shelters. Not since Joshua, who brought them into Canaan, had Israel done so. After seven days of reading the Torah, they hold a solemn assembly on the eighth day.

NEHEMIAH 9–10: A NEW COVENANT

This time, focusing on God's word leads the people to repent because they realize that their lives reflect their fathers' lives. The trauma of their current fate is a by-product of a lack of trust in God and His word. Many men, therefore, commit to follow God in a covenant that obligates them to follow the Torah's law codes, to not give their sons or daughters in marriage to the peoples of the nations, to not break the Sabbath, and to give tithes and offerings according to the Torah.

Confession in the Writings

Daniel 9, Ezra 9, and Nehemiah 9 emphasize poetic and interpretive reflections on the Torah and the Prophets. In each of these situations, God's faithfulness and Israel's failures lead Daniel, Ezra, and some of the Levites to confess their sin and the people's sin as they hope for God's mercy.

NEHEMIAH 11–12: JERUSALEM AS THE PLACE WHERE GOD DWELLS

Within Jerusalem and across the land, the priestly and Levitical families are organized to support the temple's work, marking all of Jerusalem as holy. The walls of the city are dedicated with music and choirs that allow the whole city to echo the temple's worship of God. The city of Jerusalem now reflects God's glory in a new way.

NEHEMIAH 13: THE FAILURES OF JERUSALEM AND HER PEOPLE

Unfortunately, the people violate their covenant obligations. Tobiah, who had opposed the temple, now has a room within its courts. The tithes and portions dedicated to care for the Levites are not being given. After reprimanding the leaders for their sins, Nehemiah asks God to remember his faithful deeds in these matters. The people also stop honoring the Sabbath, but Nehemiah intervenes to impose a Sabbath order on them. Again, Nehemiah asks God to remember him and show him compassion. Lastly, the people marry the women of the nations. Nehemiah rebukes them for not learning from Solomon's failings. Nehemiah asks God to remember their breaking of the covenant. He has only one hope. Nehemiah needs God to remember him for his good.

KEY TAKEAWAYS

Nehemiah leads God's people to rebuild the city's walls. Their work offers a space and a place for God to do His work in His people. Ezra reads the Torah to all the people so that God may draw them to repentance and renewal. Their response to the Scriptures leads them to make a covenant before God. However, the renewal fades over time. The people and Nehemiah find themselves waiting on God to remember His promises.

1 AND 2 CHRONICLES

A Review of the Old Testament

> "But will God in very deed dwell with men on the earth?
> behold, heaven and the heaven of heavens cannot contain thee;
> how much less this house which I have built!"
> —2 Chronicles 6:18

Both 1 and 2 Chronicles review the entire Old Testament. Beginning with genealogies that race from Adam to David, the author presents David, Solomon, and his temple as previews of the future Son of David and his work. Avoiding David's sin with Bathsheba and Solomon's sins with his many wives, the book traces the positives of their lives and the temple. He does not follow the fate of the northern kingdom, but he searches the kings of Judah to see if the Son of David has come. He has not, but He is certainly coming. 1 and 2 Chronicles adds more scenes to certain stories from Kings. After he shows the temple destroyed, the author concludes his book and the Old Testament with a shortened version of Cyrus's decree that is also in Ezra's book. This gentile king announces to the reader that we should expect the Son of David soon.

1 CHRONICLES 1–10: GENEALOGIES OF GOD'S STORY WITH HIS PEOPLE

Beginning with Adam, 1 Chronicles revisits the Old Testament's early chapters in a long genealogy that covers Adam to Abraham to David. After drawing out David's family, the author describes the genealogies of the other tribes of Israel. In the middle of this genealogy, he focuses on Aaron's family as priests from the tribe of Levi and their tabernacle work. These lists conclude with a focus on Benjamin and Saul. Saul's failures anticipate Israel's exile and pave the way for the king who will arise after Saul: David.

1 CHRONICLES 11–29: THE SON OF DAVID AND DAVID'S PLAN FOR THE TEMPLE

Beginning with David's ascension to the throne over all Israel, Jerusalem becomes its capital. It is a kingdom marked by mighty warriors for David, whom God shapes to be great leaders and fighters. After a failed attempt to bring the Ark to Jerusalem, David meditates on and abides by the Torah. He then appoints Levites to bring the Ark into the city with joy, to give thanks to God, and to lead worship in its presence.

With the Ark in place, the author returns us to 2 Samuel 7. David desires to build a house for God that surpasses his own, but God contends that his son will build an everlasting house with God. The rest of 1 Chronicles revisits this promise and shows its development in David's life, in Solomon's life, and among the people. God establishes David as a prototype of his ideal son because he rules a powerful kingdom that subdues all other nations. However, this positive portrait pauses to remind us of David's pride and sense of grandeur when he sinned by counting his fighting men in a census that was against God's wishes.

The Temple's Goals

After the census attempt, David plans for the temple that his son Solomon will build. He charges Solomon to seek discretion and understanding from God so that he may obey the Torah. The worship of God in the temple that Solomon will build will emphasize the Levites, priests, musicians, singers, and gatekeepers. They will establish worship and order in the temple and beyond it. David also appoints Solomon's military commanders, overseers, and counselors to manage his vast kingdom. The details and design of the temple's pattern are from David and given to Solomon.

Finally, David prays for the people and compels them to follow God as Solomon will lead them. The people should heed the Torah and its laws, and they should ask God to remember the promise to Abraham. After all these instructions, Solomon is made king, and David dies.

David and the Temple

David wants to build God a house, a temple, but no man can build a sufficient house to hold God. Instead, God will build David an everlasting house through the Son of David. He affirms David's intentions and lets him prepare and plan for Solomon's temple.

2 CHRONICLES 1–36: LOOKING FOR THE SON OF DAVID

The author quickly brings us to Solomon's request for God's wisdom and his labor to build the temple. The location of this temple is on Mount Moriah: the very place where Abraham prepared to sacrifice

Isaac and also the same place where David sacrificed to turn God's wrath after his census. When the construction finishes, Solomon dedicates the temple to God, and God's glory falls upon it. Solomon's kingdom is shown to be powerful, wealthy, and wiser than all other kingdoms. Without mentioning Solomon's sin, the author notes Solomon's death and leads the reader to search for the Son of David in his sons, who will rule only the southern kingdom, Judah.

As 2 Chronicles works its way through the kings of Judah, the book repeats much of 1 and 2 Kings but includes new, meaningful details. As we return to Hezekiah and Josiah, for example, we learn more of Hezekiah's reforms and Passover celebration, as well as Josiah's Passover celebration and his death. The most unexpected of these sections is Manasseh. He is the worst of all the kings of Judah, but God raises up the Assyrians to exile him in Babylon. In Babylon, Manasseh repents, and God is moved by his prayer to return him to this throne. Manasseh's journey anticipates Israel's exile and return.

After the Babylonian exile of Judah, 1 and 2 Chronicles and the Old Testament end with confidence in Jeremiah's future promise of an end to God's people's exile. The biblical author shortens the decree from the Persian king Cyrus to build the temple to focus on the hope of one man, the Son of David, coming from among His people to do what Israel cannot do on their own: "Who is there among you of all his people? The LORD his God be with him, and let him go up" (2 Chr 36:23).

KEY TAKEAWAYS

In 1 and 2 Chronicles, the author searches the kings of Judah to see if the Son of David has come. He has not, but He is certainly coming. After the temple is destroyed, the author concludes with Cyrus's decree. This gentile king announces that we should expect the Son of David soon.

NEW TESTAMENT BASICS

Understanding the New Testament's Four Major Sections

"But the word of the Lord endureth for ever."
—1 Peter 1:25

The New Testament is a collection of twenty-seven books, written two thousand years ago in Koine Greek by early Christians. The New Testament is made up of Gospels, a theological history, letters, and an apocalypse. These works were collected together over a relatively short period of time into the New Testament found in modern Bibles.

THE LAYOUT OF THE NEW TESTAMENT

The contents of the New Testament are organized into four major categories:

- The Four Gospels: Matthew, Mark, Luke, and John
- Acts: A theological history of the early Christians
- A collection of Paul's letters: Romans, 1–2 Corinthians, Galatians, Ephesians, Philippians, Colossians, 1–2 Thessalonians, 1–2 Timothy, Titus, and Philemon
- A collection of other Apostolic writings: Hebrews, James, 1–2 Peter, 1–3 John, Jude, and Revelation

Let's look at each in more detail.

The Four Gospels

The first four books of the New Testament are the Gospels (from the Greek *euangelion*, meaning "good news"). The four canonical Gospels are named after their traditional authors. Matthew and John were members of Jesus' twelve original disciples (the Apostles). Mark was the disciple of the Apostle Peter, and Luke was a missionary and the disciple of the Apostle Paul. The Gospels are collections of the teachings of Jesus and stories about him, from his birth until his resurrection.

The Mark Misinformation

In 2011, it was sensationally reported that a first-century manuscript fragment of the Gospel of Mark had been discovered. It turned out not to be quite that old—with a more likely date of between A.D. 150 and A.D. 250—but it is still the earliest surviving fragment of Mark.

Acts: A Theological History of the Early Christians

The book of Acts (from the Greek *praxeis*, meaning "deeds") is a collection of narratives about the earliest Christians in the years after the resurrection of Jesus. Acts is traditionally believed to be written by Luke, the author of the Gospel of Luke. The first half of Acts centers on the expansion of Christianity in Jerusalem and the surrounding area, and has Peter as its focal character. The second half of Acts tells of the missionary journeys of the Apostle Paul, his arrest in Jerusalem, and his imprisonment in Rome.

A Collection of Paul's Letters

The New Testament contains thirteen letters the Apostle Paul wrote during his life as a missionary. The letters of Paul are named after their destinations, either people or Christian communities. Where more than one letter was written to a single locale, the letters are also numbered (e.g., 1 Corinthians and 2 Corinthians). The book called Hebrews, though not believed by modern scholars to have been written by the Apostle Paul, is also named like one of Paul's letters, after its destination (Jewish Christians), and is placed between Paul's letters and the general letters in modern New Testaments.

A Collection of Other Apostolic Writings

The final section in the New Testament, often called the *general letters*, is a collection of writings traditionally believed to be written by other Apostles and those connected to Apostles. The general letters are named after their traditional authors and are also numbered where more than one letter is present from a single author (e.g., 1 Peter and 2 Peter).

The last of the general letters is the book of Revelation. It gets its name from its ancient title in Greek (*apokalypsis*, "to reveal"). Revelation is a Christian apocalypse—a dramatic and symbolic depiction of how God plans to bring the Kingdom of God to the earth—that follows the pattern of the apocalyptic literature in the Old Testament.

DATE AND COLLECTION

Jesus was born somewhere between 6 and 4 B.C. and likely died between A.D. 30 and 33. Most scholars believe at least some of the New Testament books were written in the A.D. 40s or 50s. The first Gospel to be written, the Gospel of Mark, could have been written in the A.D. 50s or 60s, but many scholars date it a little later, just after A.D. 70.

Historically, the writings traditionally ascribed to the Apostle John (the Gospel of John, 1–3 John, and Revelation) were believed to be the last books of the New Testament written, probably around A.D. 90, though some modern scholars have later dates for some of the other New Testament books. By A.D. 150, a significant portion of the New Testament was being referenced and quoted in other Christian writings, and manuscript fragments of copies of the New Testament started to appear in other parts of the world. This means that the New Testament was begun a decade or two after the death and resurrection of Jesus and was at least mostly finished within about sixty years.

MANUSCRIPTS AND COPIES

None of the original manuscripts of the New Testament have survived to the modern day. Thousands of copies, however, have survived, and some of them are very old, as old as the early second century. The vast majority of these copies are from books (codices), not scrolls, even if only tiny fragments of the books remain. The codex was a relatively new technology during the time of Jesus. Because of its economy and portability, the book rapidly became the preferred method of writing by the earliest Christians. As Christianity spread, so did the book's popularity, making the scroll all but obsolete.

Ancient Copies of the New Testament

There are more than five thousand extant ancient copies of the New Testament today, ranging from tiny fragments to entire Bibles. By comparison, second place is held by Homer's *Iliad* at only about six hundred fifty ancient copies. This makes the New Testament the most well-attested-to ancient work in history, by far.

Ancient Christian documents call the books of the New Testament *Scripture*. Ancient New Testaments from within one hundred years of its completion looked much like the New Testaments of today in content, though some of the books in current New Testaments are not regularly listed by ancient Christians until a bit later. By the fourth century, however, all twenty-seven books of the New Testament were present and accounted for.

KEY TAKEAWAYS

A surprising amount of data about the origins of the New Testament has survived. Scholars have a good idea of what the earliest New Testaments looked like, and though there is plenty of discussion by scholars on how the New Testament was originally collected together, it is clear that the period of collection was fairly short. The New Testament was subsequently copied with great vigor, leaving a clear paper trail for modern scholars to follow.

THE FOUR GOSPELS

The Words of Matthew, Mark, Luke, and John

> "The beginning of the gospel of Jesus Christ, the Son of God."
> —Mark 1:1

Matthew, Mark, Luke, and John are the four New Testament Gospels. They record many of the accounts of Jesus' ministry during his time on earth, and they also contain extensive amounts of Jesus' teaching. The earliest Christians believed the Gospels to be *the* authoritative witness to the good news of salvation and to the things Jesus said and did.

WHAT THE GOSPELS ARE NOT

The Gospels are not biographies. Though they do contain true biographical material about Jesus, they do not work like modern biographies. Only two of the Gospels describe Jesus' birth, and only one of the Gospels contains any information at all about the life of Jesus between his birth and his baptism some thirty years later. Instead, the Gospels focus on the adult ministry and teaching of Jesus and are presented by their authors as theological accounts of Jesus. These are theological accounts because they have been shaped by their authors to clearly identify Jesus as God, who has come to earth to be the Savior of the whole world.

Gospels versus *Gospel*

Modern scholars use the word *Gospel* (with a capital *G*) when referring to a book or books with the title of *Gospel*, as in *the Gospel of Matthew* or *the four Gospels*. Scholars also use the word *gospel* (with a lowercase *g*) when referring to the content of Jesus' teaching about himself. The word *gospel* itself can be translated as "good news" (from the Greek *euangellion*), and in the New Testament this refers to the coming of Jesus, his death for the sins of the world, and his resurrection from the dead.

Good News

Christians did not invent the word *gospel*. In the Roman era, it meant "good news" and was used to describe important news, such as a declaration of military victory, the announcement of a new emperor, or the arrival of someone important. Christians quickly adopted the word to describe the life, death, and resurrection of Jesus. (In Jesus' day, nearly all of the Roman Empire spoke Koine Greek as the common/trade language, so it is both a Greek word and within normal use in the Roman Empire.)

THE ANATOMY OF A GOSPEL

Scholars often have complex systems for classifying the material in the Gospels, but it is helpful to have at least two broad categories: narratives and teaching.

The four Gospels contain many narratives about Jesus. These stories are not told in the fashion of fables or myths. They are presented as factual accounts, and they contain many eyewitness details. Often, these narratives describe the miracles of Jesus, and sometimes they are grouped together thematically. For example, in Matthew 8–9, Matthew appears to have grouped together for his readers a collection of the miracles performed by Jesus.

The four Gospels also contain an extensive collection of the teaching of Jesus. Jesus teaches large crowds, both friendly and hostile, and Jesus teaches his disciples in private. In the Gospels, Jesus occasionally speaks on ethics and even more rarely comments on the current events of his day. The Old Testament was the "Bible" from which Jesus taught, and his teaching was theological: his identity as Messiah, salvation, and the Kingdom of God.

The Gospels and the rest of the New Testament present Jesus as the Son of God. The Scripture reveals that the one God eternally exists in three persons: Father, Son, and Holy Spirit. The Christian term for this phenomenon is *Trinity*. The Son was sent into the world by the Father and was born of the Virgin Mary by the power of the Holy Spirit to be the Savior. This event is called the *Incarnation*.

The Parables of Jesus

Jesus frequently taught in parables—short, made-up stories about everyday life that contain a spiritual message. Jesus often told his parables in a way that made them memorable and easy to pass on, using a simple, repeating story structure. Most of the time, the Gospel writers give the context in which Jesus told his parables. For example, Luke explains that Jesus spoke the Parable of the Prodigal Son to the religious leaders after they criticized him for befriending and teaching tax collectors and sinners. Jesus or the Gospel writers give clear indications as to the meaning of each parable, making them easy to understand for later readers. Parables typically have one major idea they want to communicate, though some of the longer parables, those with multiple characters, often have more than one big idea.

SIMILARITIES AND DIFFERENCES AMONG THE GOSPELS

The Gospels give some of their accounts of Jesus and his teaching so similarly that most scholars believe the Gospels share some literary interdependence (i.e., Matthew used Mark's Gospel as a source). The Gospels also tell some of their stories so differently as to appear contradictory. This phenomenon, called the *synoptic question*, is most pronounced in Matthew, Mark, and Luke.

What about the Other Gospels?

After the first century, other works with the name *Gospel* started to appear. The Gospel of Thomas was likely the first of these, written more than one hundred years after the death of Thomas the disciple. These noncanonical Gospels were named after Jesus' disciples in an attempt to bolster their credibility. That attempt largely failed, and they were rejected as frauds or forgeries.

The synoptic question is likely the result of not only the literary interdependence of the Gospels but also of the unique eyewitness contributions of the authors and their sources. The birth narrative in Luke, for example, is told from the perspective of Mary, Jesus' mother. This makes the account not incompatible with Matthew's account but still quite different from it.

The theological nature of the Gospels is also partially responsible for the synoptic phenomenon. Each of the Gospel authors selected, adapted, and arranged their accounts of Jesus and his teaching to reach a particular audience and to answer specific theological questions. For example, Matthew appears to be selecting and arranging the stories he tells about the beginning of Jesus' ministry in Matthew 3–4 in order to present the story of Jesus the way the Torah presents the story of Israel—out of Egypt, through the waters, into the wilderness, and up the mountain.

THE GOSPELS AND MODERN BIBLE SCHOLARSHIP

Thousands of books have been written on modern scholarship and the Bible. The following four sections on the Gospels are not ignorant of that scholarship, but they do not attempt to reconcile all of it. For the purposes of this book, these sections will assume the traditional view of authorship, circumstance of writing, and (where possible) date. The goal is to help people understand the message of Jesus and of the Gospel writer as presented in the texts themselves.

KEY TAKEAWAYS

In the search for the truth about Jesus, there can be little question as to the value of the four canonical Gospels. Only these four Gospels are believed to have been written within the lifetime of the eyewitnesses to Jesus. Only these four are believed to have been written by people who actually knew Jesus, and only these four form a unified theological message about Jesus that was uniformly accepted throughout Christendom from the beginning. This alone, of course, is not proof of their ultimate truthfulness, but it does make them the only logical starting place for anyone who wants to know about Jesus.

THE GOSPEL OF MATTHEW

The Life, Death, and Resurrection of Jesus

"Think not that I am come to destroy the law, or the prophets:
I am not come to destroy, but to fulfil."
—Matthew 5:17

The Gospel of Matthew is a theological history of the life, death, and resurrection of Jesus. Matthew's message is made clear through his accounts of Jesus' miracles and his sermons: Jesus is the Messiah, the Savior promised in the Old Testament. That did not, however, mean what most in Jesus' day expected it to mean.

THE GOSPEL ACCORDING TO A JEWISH TAX COLLECTOR

The name of the Gospel of Matthew's author does not appear anywhere within its text, which is not uncommon in ancient works. The Gospel is traditionally believed to be authored by Matthew, also called Levi, the Apostle and disciple of Jesus, as the ancient titles for the Gospel reflect. The Gospel could have been written in the A.D. 60s and was written after the Gospel of Mark. The author was an educated Jewish person with a great deal of firsthand information about Judaism and is identified in the Gospels as a tax collector. He is writing to other Jewish "insiders" about Jesus the Messiah.

MATTHEW'S MESSAGE

The Gospel of Matthew is organized around five discourses, or sermons, with an extended introduction and conclusion. Matthew tells a series of stories about Jesus and then gives those stories context by recounting one of Jesus' sermons. The five discourses in Matthew point the reader to Matthew's larger message. Over and over again in Matthew's Gospel, people reject Jesus' claim to be the promised Messiah because he is not behaving the way they expect God's Messiah to behave. Jesus himself is clear: He did not come to overthrow the Romans and restore Israel to its former economic and political glory. He came to suffer and die to save his people from their sins.

FIVE SERMONS OF JESUS

In Matthew 1–2, Matthew gives a genealogy for Jesus, connecting Jesus to King David and to Abraham, the ancient "father" of the Jewish people. Matthew then describes the divine virgin birth of Jesus, the visit of the Magi, and the murderous response of King Herod.

When Jesus next appears in Chapter 3, it is thirty years later, and a Jewish prophet called John the Baptist is proclaiming Jesus to be the Messiah. Jesus allows John to baptize him to identify himself with John's message. Jesus *is*, indeed, the Messiah. Jesus comes out of the water and goes into the desert to be tempted by Satan. Jesus succeeds where all before him have failed, and then he begins his ministry.

The Sermon on the Mount

Matthew ends the first series of narratives about Jesus in Matthew 5–7 with what is perhaps Jesus' greatest sermon: the Sermon on the Mount. In the sermon, Jesus proclaims the gospel of the Kingdom of God. The sermon ends with a dire warning: Not everyone who claims to know and obey God will escape God's judgment. Jesus identifies himself as the God who will judge everyone on the last day.

Jesus' Miracles

Matthew 8–9 are a collection of miracles that Jesus performed. These miracles serve to demonstrate that Jesus really is who he said he is in the Sermon on the Mount. Some of the most famous miracles of Jesus are in this collection, such as calming the storm by speaking to it and raising a little girl from the dead. This section ends with a sermon in Matthew 10 that Jesus preached to his disciples before sending them out to preach the good news.

Jesus' Conflicts and Parables

The narratives in Matthew 11–12 illustrate the rising conflict that Jesus has with the religious establishment. They refuse to believe that Jesus is the Messiah because he violates so many of their religious regulations and traditions, especially concerning Sabbath regulations, traditions that Jesus believes are keeping people from God, not helping them find Him. Jesus is not violating the Old Testament law codes; Jesus obeys the Scripture. Matthew follows these stories of conflict with a collection of parables in Matthew 13. These parables not only tell what God's Kingdom is like; they also explain why, even though Jesus is clearly God's Messiah, so many people refuse to believe in him.

The Parable in Jewish Teaching

The parable is far older than the New Testament. Jesus' use of parables was most likely inspired by their popularity among the rabbis and by the parables in the Old Testament (e.g., 2 Samuel 12:1–9), which were written hundreds of years before Matthew. The concentration of parables in the teaching of Jesus is unprecedented in the ancient world, however.

Believers and Nonbelievers

Matthew 14–17 focuses primarily on the divide between those who believe in Jesus and those who do not. Jesus works a number of famous miracles (feeding the five thousand, walking on the water, etc.), making his identity as Messiah entirely clear. The hostility of those who do not believe in him grows even stronger, but Jesus continues proclaiming the same message: The Messiah must die for the sins of the world and on the third day rise from the dead. Matthew ends this section in Chapter 18 with Jesus' sermon to his disciples on life in the Kingdom of God. Entrance into God's Kingdom is through repentance, humility, and faith.

Jesus' Final Days

Matthew 19–23, the final set of narratives, contain more teaching by Jesus as well as a description of his final days. Jesus rides into Jerusalem in fulfillment of Old Testament prophecy. He is greeted with great fervor, but instead of riding to the nearest Roman installation and starting a political revolt, Jesus rides to the temple and throws the religious leaders out. In Matthew 24–25, Jesus preaches an apocalyptic sermon about the end of days. Jesus proclaims that he himself, the Son of God, will return on the last day to judge the world.

The final chapters in Matthew, 26–28, detail the events of Jesus' final days. He eats the Last Supper with his disciples, a traditional Passover meal at which Jesus proclaims Passover to be about him. Jesus presents himself as the slain lamb who dies so that sinners might live. Jesus then prays in the garden of Gethsemane, where he is betrayed by one of his own disciples, Judas, and is arrested. Jesus is put on trial, brutally tortured, and executed by the Romans at the behest of the Jewish religious leaders. On the third day, early in the morning, Mary (perhaps the mother of Jesus) and Mary Magdalene (a follower of Jesus, who heals her of demonic possession, according to the Gospel of Luke) visit the tomb, but it is empty. Jesus has risen from the dead and commands his disciples to take the good news of the Savior to the ends of the earth.

KEY TAKEAWAYS

Though Jesus was not the Messiah most people were expecting, Matthew is clear that Jesus is the Savior promised in the Old Testament. Jesus' sermons in the Gospel make plain the good news and teach the followers of the Messiah how to live in God's Kingdom while they await the return of Jesus. The Gospel ends with a command to take the good news about Jesus beyond the confines of Israel into all the world.

THE GOSPEL OF MARK

Suffering and Discipleship

"Truly this man was the Son of God."
—Mark 15:39

The shortest of the four Gospels, Mark is a concise, action-packed presentation of Jesus as the Son of God. The focus of this Gospel is on suffering and discipleship. By describing the suffering of Jesus and the continued failure of the disciples to understand him, Mark provides instruction and encouragement for followers of Jesus for how to grow in their faith even during difficult times.

THE FIRST GOSPEL

Though not the first Gospel in the New Testament, Mark was likely the first Gospel written. The Gospel of Mark bears Mark's name, because Mark the Evangelist was consistently identified as its author for most of Christian history. Mark was not one of Jesus' original twelve disciples, but Mark the Evangelist is believed to be John Mark, the Christian missionary and disciple of the Apostle Peter described in the later New Testament. Mark could have been written as early as the A.D. 50s, but most scholars set a somewhat later date for the book. The Gospel was likely written to a Roman audience, as confirmed by the testimony of the ancient Christians and a host of textual evidence.

THE BEGINNING OF THE GOSPEL OF JESUS CHRIST, THE SON OF GOD

Mark is quite different from Matthew and Luke. It is significantly shorter, and it also does not have a birth narrative or a genealogy for Jesus. The Gospel begins with a title of sorts: "The beginning of the gospel of Jesus Christ, the Son of God" (Mark 1:1) and then races though the introductory stories about the beginning of Jesus' ministry to focus on the miracle story in Mark 2:1–12, where Jesus demonstrates himself to be the God who forgives sin.

The Gospel According to Peter?

Some ancient sources claim that Mark is an interpretation of the teaching of Peter the Apostle, probably during his time in Rome as a missionary. There is some circumstantial evidence for this claim in the New Testament, and this may account for some of the eyewitness details found in Mark.

The Gospel of Mark is also incredibly candid about the failure of the disciples to understand who Jesus is. They see Jesus work divine miracles, like speaking to the weather and the weather obeying him, just as God speaks in Genesis and creates the world. They respond with fear. Peter proclaims that Jesus is the Messiah, but the moment Jesus begins to explain how the Messiah must die for the sins of the world and rise from the dead, Peter begins to rebuke him. Even at the very end of Mark's Gospel, after Jesus has risen from the dead, the disciples are afraid and full of doubts. Mark expects his audience to identify with the spiritual failures of the disciples and be encouraged by Jesus' faithfulness to them.

MARK 1–8

Mark's Gospel can be divided into three distinct sections. The first section, Mark 1–8, begins with a brief introduction to Jesus' ministry and then moves the reader quickly through Jesus' activities in Galilee. The introduction is theological in nature. Jesus is described as the fulfillment of Old Testament prophecy, a truth that is confirmed by the preaching of John the Baptist. Mark gives only a few sentences each on the events that characterize the beginning of Jesus' ministry: Jesus' baptism, the temptation, the calling of the first disciples, and the early miracles.

Jesus' Miracles

The miraculous activity of Jesus forms the backbone of the first part of Mark's Gospel. Most of the lengthy sermons of Jesus are only excerpted in Mark's Gospel, and Mark never allows much time to pass in his account of Jesus without returning to an account of Jesus' divine power: the power to heal, the power to cast out demons, and the power to control the natural world simply by speaking to it. Like Matthew, Mark tells a story of increasing polarization. Those who refuse to believe that Jesus is the Messiah reject Jesus, often in public confrontations.

Mark's first major section ends with Jesus questioning his disciples as to his identity. Peter boldly answers: "Thou art the Christ" (Mark 8:29). It is clear from the paragraphs that follow, however, that Peter terribly misunderstands what it means for Jesus to be the Christ. Peter is appalled that Jesus would suggest that as the Messiah, he would be rejected and die; Peter rebukes Jesus, so Jesus tells the disciples to tell no one who he is. Until they correctly understand that the Messiah must die for the sins of the world and rise from the dead, Jesus does not want them as spokespersons.

MARK 9–13

The second section, Mark 9–13, is about the final days of Jesus' Galilean ministry and his time in Jerusalem before his death. Jesus continues to work miracles, and his confrontations with the religious leaders grow more frequent and more serious. After the end of Mark 13, the religious leaders are openly plotting to kill Jesus.

Once Jesus rides triumphantly into Jerusalem, he runs the money changers out of the temple. Jesus prophesies the destruction of the temple and speaks at length on how the world will end.

MARK 14–16

Jesus is arrested in Mark 14, and the final chapters, Mark 14–16, record Jesus' last days. Jesus is interrogated by the Jewish religious council, found guilty of blasphemy, and then turned over to Pilate, the Roman governor, for execution. Pilate complies out of political expediency, and Jesus is tortured and crucified. After Passover, some of Jesus' disciples visit the tomb where he was buried, only to find a "young man" (an angel, Mark 16:5) in the tomb and Jesus risen from the dead.

KEY TAKEAWAYS

From beginning to end, Mark's Gospel focuses on presenting Jesus as the Son of God, the Suffering Servant promised in the Old Testament. Mark's Gospel is candid about the failures of the disciples to understand what it means for Jesus to be the Messiah. Jesus suffers and dies for the sins of the world and rises from the dead to give hope to all of Jesus' disciples who are struggling to follow Jesus in the midst of suffering.

THE GOSPEL OF LUKE

A Non-Jewish Perspective on Jesus

"For the Son of man is come to seek and to save that which was lost."
—Luke 19:10

Luke is unique among the Gospels in that it provides a non-Jewish perspective on the life and death of Jesus the Messiah. When Jewish missionaries came to a Roman city, they brought the good news of a Jewish Messiah, promised in the Jewish Scriptures and fulfilled in Judea, the historic land of the Jewish people. Non-Jewish people likely wondered, "What does all this have to do with us?" The Gospel of Luke answers that question. Luke was written by a non-Jewish person to non-Jewish people to explain that Jesus is not just a Jewish Messiah. Jesus is the God and Savior of the whole world.

THE GENTILE GOSPEL

Like the other Gospels, the name of the author does not occur anywhere in the text of Luke. The earliest references to Luke's Gospel, however, attribute it to Luke, the physician and missionary traveling companion of Paul the Apostle. This puts the traditional date of the Gospel's production during or shortly after Paul's imprisonment in the early A.D. 60s, though modern scholars have suggested a wide variety of theories as to authorship and date. Luke is part one of a two-part work with Acts. Together, they make up more than one-fourth of the New Testament.

In What Order Were the Gospels Written?

Modern scholars generally believe Mark to be the first Gospel written because it appears that both Matthew and Luke use Mark as a source. Though there is some debate as to whether Luke or Matthew came next, there is vast agreement that John's Gospel was written last, probably decades later.

The Gospel of Luke is addressed to a man named Theophilus, a non-Jewish person and probably a new convert to Christianity. Luke calls him "most excellent" (Luke 1:3) (*kratistos* in Greek), a term used for other Roman officials in the New Testament, indicating that Theophilus might be a public servant of some sort.

A GOSPEL FOR THEOPHILUS

Throughout Luke's Gospel, especially in his central section (Luke 9–19), Luke focuses on the stories, teaching, and parables of Jesus that feature non-Jewish people, outcasts, Roman employees, women, and other people who are marginalized in society. Luke is selecting, adapting, and arranging the material about Jesus in a way that lets Theophilus and other non-Jewish readers see themselves in the life and ministry of Jesus.

THE MESSAGE OF LUKE

Like Matthew, Luke begins his Gospel with narratives about Jesus' birth in Luke 1–2. These narratives are told primarily from the perspective of Mary, the mother of Jesus. Luke also has a genealogy of

Jesus, but he puts it at the end of Chapter 3. Luke's genealogy traces Jesus' family tree in a way that links Jesus to Adam, connecting the Savior not just to Jewish figures but to all mankind.

In Luke 3–5, Luke gives the same basic introduction to Jesus' ministry as Matthew and Mark. Jesus is baptized by John. Jesus overcomes Satan's temptations in the wilderness. Jesus preaches in the synagogues, works some early miracles, and calls the first disciples.

Jesus' Ministry in Galilee

Jesus arrives in Galilee in Chapter 4, and Luke's account of Jesus' ministry in Galilee also follows a similar pattern to Matthew and Mark. Luke, however, does not miss a chance to highlight stories that involve non-Jewish people, Roman officials, or societal outcasts. In Luke 5, Jesus heals five lepers, and calls a tax collector (Matthew) to be his disciple. In Luke 7, Jesus heals the servant of a centurion (a Roman military officer) and offers forgiveness to a "sinful woman" (a sex worker). The Galilean ministry ends in Chapter 9 with Jesus preaching the gospel in a Samaritan village (the political and religious enemies of Israel) before beginning the journey to Jerusalem.

The Travel Narrative

Jesus' journey to Jerusalem is told over eleven chapters in Luke 9–19. Scholars call this lengthy central section the *travel narrative* because it begins with Jesus deciding to go to Jerusalem and ends when he arrives there in Chapter 19. This section makes up about 40 percent of the Gospel and includes most of the material that is unique to Luke's Gospel. This section appears to be specifically designed for Theophilus and other non-Jewish readers.

The travel narrative contains mostly teaching material with a few miracles and a substantial number of parables that are not recorded in

Matthew and Mark. In Chapter 10, Jesus unfavorably compares Israel with non-Jewish cities and makes a Samaritan the hero of a parable. In Chapter 11, Jesus compares his ministry to the ministry of the prophet Jonah, who was called by God to preach to non-Jewish people. In Chapter 14, Luke tells a pair of parables that explain the gospel and what God will do when Israel rejects the Messiah—He will create for Himself a people from all the nations. In Chapter 18, Jesus tells a parable in which a Roman employee rightly responds to God's mercy, and in Chapter 19, Jesus befriends a notoriously corrupt tax collector named Zacchaeus.

Luke ends his Gospel in a fashion similar to Matthew and Mark. In Chapter 19, Jesus rides into Jerusalem and receives a grand reception, but after Jesus runs the money changers out of the temple, the public confrontations with the religious establishment begin. In Chapters 20–21, Jesus teaches his disciples, foretells the destruction of the temple, and preaches on the end of the world. In Chapter 22, Jesus eats the Passover with his disciples, is betrayed by Judas, and is arrested in the garden of Gethsemane. Jesus is put on trial, tortured, and executed in Chapter 23, and Jesus rises from the dead and appears, after his resurrection, to his disciples in Chapter 24. The Gospel ends with Jesus explaining the mission of the Messiah to his disciples: "that repentance and remission of sins should be preached in his name among all nations" (Luke 24:47).

KEY TAKEAWAYS

Local religions were common in the Roman world, and new sects sprang up all the time. Luke wants Theophilus and all his readers to know that Christianity is not just another local Jewish sect. Christianity is good news for the whole world, which is why Christians take the gospel of Jesus into the whole world.

THE GOSPEL OF JOHN

Discovering and Growing Faith

"For God so loved the world, that he gave his only begotten Son, that whosoever believeth in him should not perish, but have everlasting life."
—John 3:16

The Gospel of John is clear about its purpose. It was written "that
ye might believe that Jesus is the Christ, the Son of God; and that
believing ye might have life through his name" (John 20:31). This
is not just evangelism; it is also discipleship. The Gospel of John
wants its readers to believe in Jesus for the first time, and it wants its
readers to grow deeper in their faith.

THE LAST OF THE GOSPELS

The Gospel of John is the last of the Gospels and comes decades
after Matthew, Mark, and Luke. John is traditionally attributed to
John the Apostle, one of Jesus' original disciples. If John is the
author, then the Gospel was written near the end of John's life, in
the late A.D. 80s or early 90s. There is a great deal of language in
the Gospel of John that confirms that it was written significantly
later than the other Gospels.

IN THE BEGINNING WAS THE WORD: AN OVERVIEW

In order to accomplish the goal of the purpose statement in 20:31, John divides his Gospel into two halves. The first half is made up of the "signs" chapters. John, after a brief theological introduction to Jesus, organizes his narrative of the ministry of Jesus around seven signs. These signs are the deeds of Jesus, usually miraculous, and they grow in how spectacular they are as the Gospel progresses, beginning with Jesus turning water into wine in John 2 and ending with the raising of Lazarus from the dead in Chapter 11.

The second half of John's Gospel is made up primarily of the teaching of Jesus and the passion narratives. Before his arrest and execution, Jesus prepares his disciples for his death, resurrection, and ultimate departure back into heaven. John ends with an epilogue that gives a theological summation to the Gospel.

Running across both halves of John are a number of "I am" statements. Jesus uses seven different "I am" metaphors to help his hearers understand his identity. Occasionally, Jesus uses unqualified "I am" statements (e.g., "Before Abraham was, I am," John 8:58) to identify himself with the name of God and the God who speaks from the burning bush in Exodus 3.

THE MESSAGE OF JOHN

Instead of a series of birth narratives, John begins his Gospel with a theological explanation of Jesus. John calls Jesus the "Word" (e.g., John 1:1), a reference to God's word and God's presence in the Old

Testament, and says that Jesus was with God, and Jesus was God. Then John explains that God became flesh (in the person of Jesus) and lived a glorious life on earth.

Seven Signs

In John 2–11, John offers his readers seven signs that Jesus is the Son of God, God made flesh. Jesus turns the water into wine at a wedding in Galilee, and he runs the religious hypocrites out of the temple in Chapter 2. In Chapter 4, Jesus heals an official's son simply by saying, "Go thy way; thy son liveth" (John 4:50). In Chapter 5, Jesus heals a man who cannot walk at the pool of Bethesda in Jerusalem, and in Chapter 6, Jesus feeds five thousand families by multiplying the lunch of one boy. In Chapter 9, Jesus heals a man who was born blind, and in John 11, he raises Lazarus after he had been dead for so long his corpse was starting to smell.

In each of these signs, Jesus makes his identity clear. Some people see these signs and believe in Jesus, and others see these signs and grow increasingly angrier at Jesus. But everyone knows exactly who Jesus is.

"I Am" Statements

In John 6–15, John records the seven metaphorical "I am" statements of Jesus to help the reader understand who Jesus is. In John 6, Jesus calls himself the "bread of life," and in Chapters 8 and 9, Jesus calls himself the "light of the world." These metaphors identify Jesus as divine and as the gifts of God: spiritual food and the revelation of God Himself. In Chapter 10, Jesus calls himself the "gate of the sheep pen" and the "good shepherd." The sheep are meant to represent the followers of Jesus. God gives them spiritual protection, and Jesus cares for them like a shepherd cares for the sheep.

In Chapter 11, Jesus calls himself the "resurrection and the life." Jesus is the one who gives eternal life, and is the one who will raise the dead on the last day. Jesus calls himself the "way, the truth, and the life" and the "true vine" in Chapters 14 and 15, respectively. Both of these speak to the exclusivity of Jesus in salvation. There is no knowing God apart from Jesus. There is no salvation apart from Jesus, and just as the branch cannot live apart from the vine, so people cannot truly live apart from Jesus.

The Pharisees, Sadducees, and Herodians

The three major Jewish parties in Jesus' day were the Pharisees, the Sadducees, and the Herodians. By the writing of John, however, the Sadducees and the Herodians effectively no longer existed. John rarely distinguishes between these groups in his Gospel, preferring simply to call them all "the Jews."

The Epilogue

After recounting the passion of Jesus—the Passover meal, the betrayal and arrest, and Jesus' trials—John ends his Gospel with an epilogue. This epilogue begins with his purpose statement in 20:31, which is followed by a series of narratives in which Jesus continues to restore his disciples after they abandon him, and a parting note about the amazing volume of the miraculous things Jesus did.

KEY TAKEAWAYS

Everyone in the Gospel of John who encounters Jesus walks away knowing exactly who Jesus is. Even those who reject the message of Jesus know that he is the Messiah, the Son of God—but they reject him anyway. John wants to put his readers in that same dilemma. John makes it abundantly clear who Jesus is and then calls his readers to respond, not by rejecting the Savior but by believing in him.

ACTS

The Early Days of the Christian Church

"And ye shall be witnesses unto me both in Jerusalem, and in all Judaea, and in Samaria, and unto the uttermost part of the earth."

—Acts 1:8

The book of Acts tells the story of the early days of the Christian church. The author has selected and arranged the accounts of numerous historical events to proclaim a theological truth—namely, the success of Jesus' mission to take the gospel out of Jerusalem and to the "uttermost parts of the earth" (Acts 1:8).

LUKE, PART TWO

Scholars generally agree that the person who wrote Luke also wrote Acts as a companion volume. The two books share parallel introductions. They are written to the same person (Theophilus), and their style and vocabulary are similar. Near the end of Acts (e.g., Acts 16:10–17), the narrative switches from the third person ("They went," "they had") to the first person ("we sought," "we remained"), leading many scholars to conclude that the author was a some-time traveling companion of Paul the Apostle. Church history and tradition identify the author as Luke, the disciple of Paul. If true, then Acts was written in the early A.D. 60s, while Paul was in prison in Rome.

JERUSALEM, JUDEA, AND SAMARIA... AND THE ENDS OF THE EARTH

The first twelve chapters of Acts primarily concern the Apostle Peter and the first Christians in Jerusalem and the surrounding areas. The events described in Acts 1–12 take place during the first two decades after the death of Jesus.

The Christian Church in Jerusalem

Acts 1–5 focus on the church in Jerusalem. Chapter 1 picks up where the Gospel of Luke ends. Jesus repeats his mission instructions and then ascends into heaven. In Acts 2, the Holy Spirit descends upon the first Christians, and they are empowered to be Jesus' witnesses. Acts 3–5 tell about the Christians in Jerusalem, describing the miracles they worked in Jesus' name, the violent response of the local authorities, and God's intervention on their behalf. Throughout the city of Jerusalem, Christians preach the gospel of Jesus. Thousands believe, but many respond negatively, just as they did to the teaching of Jesus.

The Christian Church in Judea and Samaria

The gospel moves outward from Jerusalem into the larger regions of Judea and Samaria in Acts 6–9. In Acts 6, the Jewish Christian church must overcome some of its early prejudices, and a man named Stephen is arrested for being a Christian. In Acts 7, Stephen preaches a sermon about Jesus from the Old Testament to his persecutors, and he is dragged out of the city and murdered. A young man named Saul (who will later become Paul the Christian missionary and Apostle) is present for the stoning of Stephen. Saul takes up the mantle of persecuting Jewish people who have converted to Christianity.

In Acts 8, a man named Philip goes to Samaria, the land of the historic enemy of the Jewish people, to preach the gospel. God works many miracles in Samaria at the hand of Philip, and many Samaritans believe in Jesus. Saul has a vision of Christ in Acts 9, a major turning point in the book of Acts. There on the Damascus Road, Saul becomes a Christian. Almost immediately, he begins doing missionary work.

A Global Mission

Acts 10–12 lay the foundation for the Christian global mission that has lasted for two thousand years. In Acts 10, Peter is confronted by God with the reality that it has been more than a decade since the death of Jesus and the Christians have not truly been obedient to the mission of Jesus, because there is great reluctance on the part of the Jewish Christians to consistently preach the gospel among the gentiles. God sends Peter to the house of a Roman centurion, and Peter preaches to him the message of Jesus. The centurion and his whole household believe in Jesus.

When Peter returns to Jerusalem to explain to the other Christians there what has happened—non-Jewish people have believed in Jesus and are now the people of God too—the other Christians are reluctant to believe it. But Saul and Barnabas believe it, and in Chapter 13, they are sent from Antioch to Cyprus as missionaries. Saul changes his name to Paul.

The Spread of Christianity via Roman Roads

The Roman system of roads dates to as early as 300 B.C. The Roman Empire built 250,000 miles of roads in its day. These roads made the missionary travels of early Christians much more efficient and made the rapid delivery of the Christian Scripture around the known world possible.

The second major section of Acts, Acts 13–20, is concerned with the missionary journeys of Paul the Apostle. These events take place over about thirty years, from the mid-40s until the late 60s.

Paul's first missionary journey is to Asia Minor (Turkey), specifically to the Roman province of Galatia. After returning to Antioch from Asia Minor, Paul learns that false teachers have come in behind him in Galatia and are persuading the Christians there of a false gospel. This false gospel also spread outside of Galatia, so the other Apostles in Jerusalem call a meeting to settle the issue of what Jesus actually taught about salvation. The council concludes that salvation is by the grace of God and faith in Jesus and nothing else.

Paul then embarks on his second missionary journey to Greece and spends time in the eastern Mediterranean on his third missionary journey.

In Acts 21, Paul is preparing to go to Spain on a fourth missionary journey, but he is directed by God to return to Jerusalem. He is arrested there by Roman officials for being the subject of a local riot. Paul is jailed in Jerusalem and then Caesarea and is questioned by several Roman officials in Acts 22–26. Paul, believing that he might be killed while in custody, appeals his case to Caesar, and in Acts 27, he sets sail for Rome. The book of Acts ends with Paul in prison in Rome, preaching the gospel from house arrest to anyone who will listen.

KEY TAKEAWAYS

The ending of Acts feels abrupt because it does not tell what happened to Paul. Though Luke surely knew Paul's fate, describing the life of Paul was not his purpose. Luke ends his book when he does because he has told the story of the followers of Jesus successfully embarking on the Great Commission, which Jesus gave to his disciples to take the gospel to the ends of the earth.

PAUL AND HIS TRAVELS

The Missionary Apostle

"For I am the least of the apostles…because I persecuted the church of God.
But by the grace of God I am what I am."
—1 Corinthians 15:9–10

The book of Acts introduces Paul the Apostle and missionary. What follows in the New Testament is a collection of thirteen letters Paul wrote, now considered sacred Scripture by Christians. Paul believed that Jesus was the fulfillment of God's promise in the Old Testament of a Savior and believed himself to be chosen by God to bring the good news of the Savior to the world. Before we look at each of those letters, it will be helpful to review what we know about Paul and his life.

PAUL'S BEGINNINGS

Paul was born with the name Saul in Tarsus in Asia Minor (Turkey). He was a devout Jewish person and well educated. Paul worked for the local Jewish government, arresting Jewish people who had converted to Christianity. Luke describes Paul as enthusiastic to do his duty—"breathing out threatenings and slaughter against the disciples of the Lord" (Acts 9:1). Paul was present for at least one vicious public execution.

When Was Paul Born?

Most scholars suggest a birthdate for Paul between 5 B.C. and A.D. 5, putting him near seventy at his death. In Acts 7, however, Paul is called a young man (*neanias* in Greek). These words may indicate that he was as young as twenty there, making his birth year closer to A.D. 14.

PAUL BECOMES A CHRISTIAN

It is during one of Paul's excursions to arrest Christian converts that he encounters the risen Christ and becomes a Christian himself. Paul describes his own conversion in several places (e.g., Acts 22:3–21, Galatians 1:12–24), and Luke recounts the event in Acts 9:1–19. While on the Damascus road, Paul is surrounded by a bright light and temporarily blinded. Jesus speaks to Paul out of the light and identifies himself as the very one that Paul was persecuting. Paul believes.

Immediately following Paul's conversion, he is surrounded by local Jewish Christians who take him in. God restores Paul's sight, and Paul changes his name to Saul. He immediately begins to preach in Jewish synagogues and in the regions around Damascus that Jesus is the Son of God.

PAUL'S MISSIONARY TRAVELS

Paul wants to preach the gospel in places where it is not known. This puts him on a mostly east-to-west trajectory around the Mediterranean. According to Acts, Paul starts in Asia Minor (Turkey), moves to Greece and then to Rome, and he also wants to go to Spain. When Paul moves to a new region, he usually visits the largest cities first, where he begins his preaching in the Jewish synagogues. Paul preaches that Jesus is the Messiah promised in the Scriptures. It is during these missionary travels that Paul writes his missionary letters: Galatians, 1–2 Thessalonians, 1–2 Corinthians, and Romans.

Paul's Physical Appearance

Nothing is said of Paul's appearance in the New Testament. There are a number of later Christian sources, however, most of which are apocryphal (meaning, they are written by people who are simply repeating what they have heard and should not be taken very seriously), that do offer descriptions of Paul.

PAUL AT THE END OF HIS LIFE

After completing his third missionary journey, Paul returns to Jerusalem and is arrested there for causing a riot. He endures a series of interrogations and imprisonments, and spends time incarcerated in Jerusalem, Caesarea, and Rome. While in prison in Rome, Paul writes four more letters: Ephesians, Philippians, Colossians, and Philemon.

The book of Acts ends with Paul under house arrest in Rome awaiting his hearing. Paul's mission to get the gospel to the ends of the earth is still going strong, even from a prison cell.

It appears that Paul is eventually released from prison and that he begins his fourth missionary journey to Spain. Before heading west, Paul does some traveling in the eastern Mediterranean, and establishes two of his disciples, Timothy and Titus, to be his representatives in his absence. He writes each of them a letter (1 Timothy and Titus) and then heads to Spain.

At some point, Paul is rearrested and reimprisoned. He writes a second letter to Timothy in which Paul expects that his death is near. It is generally believed that Paul was executed during the reign of Emperor Nero, probably around A.D. 67.

PAUL AND THE TEACHING OF JESUS

Though Paul never quotes the sayings of Jesus from the Gospels in his letters, he makes numerous specific references to Jesus' teaching throughout (e.g., 1 Corinthians 7:10, 11:23–25; Romans 12:14, 14:1–4).

Modern scholars have raised questions about why so much of Jesus' teaching and details about Jesus' life are missing in Paul's letters. When Paul begins writing his letters, none of the Gospels have been written, so quoting them would have been impossible. Also, Paul is writing to Christian converts, mostly non-Jewish people, who need help understanding and applying the gospel to their contexts. The circumstances and audiences for Paul's letters are very different than the circumstances and audiences for the Gospels and for the original teaching of Jesus. This probably explains much of the seeming disconnect between the writings of Paul and the teaching of Jesus. Christian scholars throughout the centuries have found the teachings of Paul and of the Gospel writers to be entirely complementary.

THE INTEGRITY OF PAUL'S COLLECTION

From almost the very beginning, Paul's letters were gathered together and circulated as a collection. The oldest surviving manuscript of Paul's letters is one of these collections (called "Papyrus 46," ~ A.D. 175–225). It is not known exactly when Paul's letters were collected or by whom, but there was a strong tradition in the ancient world for the author himself to collect and curate his own correspondence. There is no reason why Paul would not have done the same. It may be that in 2 Timothy 4:13, when Paul requests that Timothy bring "the books, especially the parchments," Paul wants to be sure that all his letters are in one place before his death.

Some modern scholars believe that at least some of the letters of Paul in the New Testament are forgeries. The sections that follow in *Bible 101*, however, attempt to explain what the letters say and the context in which the letters themselves purport to be written. For simplicity, Paul is named as the author of all the letters that bear his name, and when the letter itself describes the circumstances around which it was written, those statements are taken at face value.

KEY TAKEAWAYS

There is no person, aside from Jesus himself, who has had greater influence on Christianity than Paul. He wrote almost half the books in the New Testament, and he pioneered the Christian missionary movement. Paul established the common vocabulary by which Christians still talk about their faith, and his lasting influence cannot be overstated.

ROMANS

Paul's Description of the Essential Doctrines of Christianity

> "For the wages of sin is death; but the gift of God
> is eternal life through Jesus Christ our Lord."
> —Romans 6:23

Paul's letter to the Romans has often been described as his magnum opus. Like most of Paul's letters, Romans was occasioned by a specific set of circumstances, but readers will find in Romans Paul's most systematic presentation of his understanding of Jesus, the gospel, salvation, and the Great Commission.

PREPARATION FOR THE MISSION TO SPAIN

Romans was written near the end of Paul's third missionary journey, probably around A.D. 56 while Paul was back in the city of Corinth. According to the book of Acts, Paul is about to return to Jerusalem (Acts 20–21) and is planning a fourth missionary journey to Spain. Since Rome is a strategic departure point for the missionaries, Paul writes the Roman Christians a letter ahead of his visit to prepare them for his arrival and to enlist their help in getting to Spain (e.g., Romans 15:24).

Christianity in Rome

Long before Paul wrote his letter to the Romans (~A.D. 57), there were sizeable Christian communities already in Rome. Converts to Christianity in other parts of the Mediterranean world brought their faith with them to Rome as lay missionaries in obedience to Jesus' mission, and new communities naturally sprang up there.

JEWISH PEOPLE, GENTILES, AND THE MISSION OF GOD

Paul wants to be sure the Christians in Rome are unified in their understanding of the gospel and of Jesus' mission. When Paul first set out on his missionary journeys a decade before, the vast majority of all the Christians in the world were Jewish. But by the time of the writing of Romans, Jewish Christians are a significant minority. Paul has already seen churches split over misunderstandings between Jewish tradition and the gospel (e.g., the Galatians) and thus writes Romans to be sure that Christians in such a strategic city properly understand both the gospel and the mission of Jesus.

According to Jesus, it is the responsibility of his followers to take the good news of salvation to the ends of the earth. Paul is convinced that divisions in the church, especially cultural and racial divisions, will hinder their understanding of the gospel and of the mission of Jesus.

THE LOGIC OF SALVATION
AND MISSION

Paul begins his description of the gospel by explaining the total and pervasive sinfulness of all humans. In Romans 1, Paul focuses on the historical sins of the pagan Romans, especially idolatry and sexual sins. In Romans 2, Paul focuses on the traditional sins of the religious Jewish people—hypocrisy and judgmentalism. Humans need to be saved from their sins. Being "pagan" cannot save them. Being "irreligious" cannot save them. And even religious activity cannot save them. Paul pushes toward the conclusions for Jewish people and gentiles: "For all have sinned, and come short of the glory of God" (Romans 3:23).

Jesus Is the Savior Humans Need

If all humans are sinners, and they are incapable of saving themselves, then all humans need a Savior. This salvation is the "righteousness of God" that comes by faith in Jesus (Romans 3:21–22). Righteousness is what people need in order to receive salvation and escape God's judgment, but righteousness is precisely what they do not have. So how do they get it? Jesus provided it by dying on the cross for the sins of the world, and people receive the righteousness of God as a gift when they believe in Jesus. This is not some new idea, Paul insists. This is what the Bible has always taught about salvation, going all the way back to Abraham from the Old Testament book of Genesis.

The Results of Salvation

In Romans 6–8, Paul discusses the day-to-day realities of what it means to believe in and follow Jesus. Those who have believed in Jesus and received the righteousness of God are no longer enslaved to sin. God empowers them to live righteously. Jesus' followers, however, do still sin and disobey God. Paul himself acknowledges that doing the right thing is not always easy. "What I hate, that do I," Paul says, and "when I would do good, evil is present with me" (Romans 7:15, 21). Consequently, those who have believed in Jesus must strive to live like Jesus. "There is therefore now no condemnation to them which are in Christ Jesus," Paul says, "who walk not after the flesh, but after the Spirit" (Romans 8:1). Paul then details all of God's daily care for his people, including his constant forgiveness, and concludes, "If God be for us, who can be against us?" (Romans 8:31).

Israel, God's Sovereignty, and Salvation

In Romans 9–11, Paul tackles some tough questions probably from the Jewish Christians in Rome, questions like: "Is it fair that God is now bestowing on gentiles the kinds of blessings he once bestowed on Israel?"; "What responsibility do Christians have toward Jewish people, especially those who have rejected Jesus?"; and "Has God replaced Israel with the gentiles as the people of God?" Though this is some of the most difficult material in all of Paul's letters to understand, Paul's larger conclusions are easy to glean. God is a God of mercy, and He is seeking after all the nations, Jewish people and gentiles, to be saved by faith in Jesus. This should not come as a surprise to anyone, least of all Israel. Christians have the same responsibility to Jewish people as they do to the whole world—everyone deserves a chance to hear the gospel, but they will only hear if Christians go and tell. And God has not ultimately cast away *any* people: "For whosoever shall call upon the name of the Lord shall be saved" (Romans 10:13).

Love As God Loves

In Chapters 12–16, Paul concludes Romans with practical examples of what it means to follow Jesus. Paul calls the Roman Christians to love as God loves. He admonishes them to obey the government as best they can and to live in such a way that their behavior does not cause others to stumble in their faith. Romans ends with a reminder of Christ's mission and a brief discussion of Paul's travel plans.

The Structure of a Pauline Letter

Most of Paul's letters, broadly speaking, have two parts. In the first part, which is usually the longest, Paul discusses theology—doctrines of God, man, sin, salvation, and the like. In the second part, Paul then explains and gives examples of how people who truly believe Christian theology live their lives.

KEY TAKEAWAYS

Christians throughout the centuries have found in Romans Paul's most comprehensive discussions of the essential doctrines of Christianity. With lawyer-like precision, Paul walks his readers through the logic of Christian theology, especially the doctrine of salvation, and leaves a lasting record of what the earliest Christians believed about Jesus and his gospel.

1–2 CORINTHIANS

Paul Corrects a Struggling Church

"That ye all speak the same thing, and that there be no divisions among you; but that ye be perfectly joined together in the same mind and in the same judgment."
—1 Corinthians 1:10

Both 1 and 2 Corinthians are some of Paul's most confrontational letters. The Corinthian churches were struggling with a number of issues, and Paul tackles them head-on in his letters. Paul's responses to the Corinthians are direct and forceful but also patient and informative.

CONFLICT WITH THE CORINTHIANS

Paul first visited the Corinthians on his second missionary journey around A.D. 50. After leaving Macedonia, Paul traveled south and landed in the city of Corinth. He preached the gospel in Corinth and helped establish a number of Christian communities there.

Some years later (~A.D. 53), while Paul was in Ephesus on his third missionary journey, he received news of the problems present in the churches in Corinth, most notoriously a sexual sin in the church—a man was apparently in an open sexual relationship with his step-mother (as described in 1 Corinthians 5:1–2). As a result, Paul writes them a series of letters, two of which were kept by Paul in his collection and thus preserved by the church. These preserved letters are called 1 and 2 Corinthians.

In 1 Corinthians, Paul writes to the churches in Corinth to instruct them on how to deal with the issue of sexual immorality as well as addressing a host of other issues related to their spiritual maturity and divisiveness. Paul is clear and direct, but the problems in Corinth persist.

By A.D. 54 or 55, Paul visited the Corinthians a second time, and it proved to be a very confrontational visit. He then writes 2 Corinthians. There is still tension between the Corinthian Christians and Paul, but their relationship is improving, and 2 Corinthians is conciliatory in nature.

A Beautiful Description of Love

1 Corinthians 13 is often called *the love chapter* and is frequently read at weddings. In it, Paul uses God's love for His creation as a model for how Christians are to love other people. Like God, love is patient and kind, and like God, love never fails.

THE CONTENT OF THE CORINTHIAN CORRESPONDENCE

In 1 Corinthians 1–4, Paul calls the Corinthians to unity in their personal relationships, in their mission to help spread the gospel of Jesus, and in their doctrine. The Christians there were divided and apparently in conflict a great deal.

Paul deals with two specific disorders in the church in 1 Corinthians 5–6. In Chapter 5, Paul addresses the aforementioned case of sexual immorality and instructs the Christians on how to deal with a person who claims Christianity but openly repudiates the teaching of Jesus. That person has already left the church in spirit, Paul argues, and the other Christians do him harm by pretending he is still a part of the church. He is to be put out of the church. In Chapter 6, Paul addresses the issue of Christians suing one another in secular court over church matters. Paul tells them he is ashamed of their poor judgment. They can and should be handling these matters themselves.

Paul answers questions about singleness, marriage, divorce, and remarriage in 1 Corinthians 7, and in 1 Corinthians 8–11, Paul answers questions about how Christians should think about their interactions with pagan culture, especially related to food, holidays, and dress. Paul's ultimate conclusion is this: When Christians decide how much of the culture they will engage with, they must prioritize obedience to Christ, love for one another, and Christ's mission.

In 1 Corinthians 12–14, Paul discusses the regular gathering of believers (i.e., the church service) and the use of "spiritual gifts" (1 Corinthians 12:1). The Corinthians were engaged in a number of common religious practices: preaching, prophetic declarations, ecstatic utterances (e.g., "speaking in tongues"). Paul encourages them to do things "decently and in order" (1 Corinthians 14:40) because that is the most loving thing to do, and it is the best way to ensure that people who do not know about Jesus can come into the assembly and hear the gospel.

Paul concludes 1 Corinthians by discussing the importance of the resurrection of Jesus (1 Corinthians 15). If Jesus did not rise from the dead as a fact of history, Paul argues, then Christianity is useless (1 Corinthians 15:14). But Jesus *did* rise from the dead, and he offers the forgiveness of sins and eternal life to everyone who believes. In 1 Corinthians 16, Paul discusses with the Corinthians his plans to continue the mission in Greece and Asia Minor (Turkey).

Paul picks up his discussion of his plans and updates the Corinthians on his situation in 2 Corinthians 1. Paul then spends the bulk of 2 Corinthians explaining to the Corinthians what a genuine life of ministry looks like. Christians endure suffering so that they can then comfort other people who are suffering. Christians accomplish Christ's mission with great boldness because they do not fear death. Christians do not lose heart, regardless of the difficulty, because they know they have eternal life. Christians see themselves as ambassadors for Christ, because God proclaims His good news through them, and Christians live lives of holiness, because their bodies are the temple of God's Spirit.

In 2 Corinthians 8–9, Paul gives principles of generosity as he reminds them of the money the Christians are collecting for relief of the Christians in Jerusalem. Just as God was generous to the whole world by sending his Son, so Christians should respond with generosity to those in need.

Paul finishes 2 Corinthians by defending his own ministry decisions and dealing with some issues of false teaching in the church. Paul warns about believing in "another gospel" (2 Corinthians 11:4) and another Jesus, meaning a different, incorrect understanding of Jesus and salvation, and he gives the Corinthians some more of his personal story, reminding them of his concern for them. Paul concludes with a final warning and greeting.

KEY TAKEAWAYS

Though 1 and 2 Corinthians are stern and confrontational, Paul wants only to help this troubled group of believers to better follow Jesus. The issues the Corinthians struggle with are relevant to churches today—bickering, immaturity, morality, and culture—and Paul calls them to unity, godliness, generosity, and mission.

GALATIANS

Jesus' Salvation

> "I marvel that ye are so soon removed from him that called you
> into the grace of Christ unto another gospel."
> —Galatians 1:6

Galatians is probably the very first of Paul's letters chronologically, though it sits after 2 Corinthians in modern Bibles, and it captures the heart of Paul's theology. The only hope for sinful mankind is a righteousness that comes from God and is credited to His people as a gift by faith in Jesus Christ. Galatians was written by Paul to a community of fledgling churches in Galatia, after he had done missionary work among them.

THE GOSPEL GOES TO GALATIA

Prior to the late nineteenth century, it was generally believed that the Galatians in the New Testament were an ethnic people group that lived in the north of Turkey. It is now frequently argued that the Galatians who received Paul's letter occupied a more southern locale, the Roman province of Galatia. Though there is still some scholarly debate over these issues, it is most likely that Paul traveled through the southern Roman province of Galatia on his first missionary journey and then, shortly after returning to Syrian Antioch, wrote the Galatians letter, probably sometime around A.D. 49.

Finding Galatia

The travels and investigations of Scottish archaeologist and biblical scholar Sir William Ramsay (1851–1939) uncovered the early Roman maps that identified the probable location of the Galatians. Ramsay's life of scholarship as an archaeologist left him entirely convinced of the historical reliability of the New Testament.

NO OTHER GOSPEL

After his first missionary journey through southern Asia Minor (Turkey), Paul returned to Syrian Antioch to prepare for his next voyage. In Antioch, Paul discovered that false teachers who were preaching a different gospel had moved in among the churches of Galatia after he left. Paul describes them as those who rely on the "works of the law" for righteousness (Galatians 3:10), and Acts 15 describes them as those who teach that circumcision (and, by extension, obedience to the other Jewish law codes in the Torah) is necessary for salvation. Paul condemns this false gospel and makes an impassioned argument for salvation as a gift of God based on faith in Jesus and not by obedience to the law codes.

AN ARGUMENT FOR SALVATION BY FAITH ALONE

Paul opens his letter in Galatians 1 with a stern confrontation. Paul accuses the Galatian Christians of abandoning the true message of Jesus, which Paul assures them was a message that he received from Jesus himself.

The Galatians have instead believed the false gospel of the so-called Judaizers. Paul reminds his readers of his extensive Jewish credentials. If anyone would know how to properly understand the place of the Old Testament in the life of a believer in the Messiah, it is Paul.

Rituals Do Not Equal Faith

In Galatians 2, Paul recounts two stories, one of a non-Jewish missionary named Titus and another about Peter the Apostle. Titus is not a Jewish person and therefore is not circumcised. Titus traveled with the other missionaries who were Jewish Christians, and not one of them suggested that Titus needed to be circumcised in order to be a Christian. Even when the missionaries went to Jerusalem and met with the Jewish disciples of Jesus, none of them suggested that Titus needed to be circumcised.

Paul confronts Peter, another Apostle who is in the area doing missionary work, over his hypocritical behavior. Peter is living and eating among the gentiles in violation of Jewish custom until more traditional Jewish believers arrive, and Peter separates himself from the gentile believers to avoid a conflict. Paul offers these accounts to the Galatians as clear evidence that becoming Jewish in practice is not what Jesus taught, nor is it how people are considered righteous before God, contrary to what the false teachers are teaching.

A Christian View of Circumcision

Paul is not opposed to circumcision and makes no comment about what is now the modern medical practice of circumcision. For Paul, the Judaizers' practice of circumcision is a false gospel. Righteousness and salvation are gifts from God that come only through faith in Christ and not through ritual observance, especially circumcision.

Living Out the Life of Christ

In Chapter 3, Paul makes a biblical argument that righteousness and salvation come by faith in Jesus and not by good works. Paul argues that contained in the story of Abraham, all the way back in Genesis 15, is an explanation of how salvation worked then and works now. Abraham "believed in the Lord" and God "counted it to him for righteousness" (Genesis 15:6). This is how anyone can be considered righteous by God—by faith (belief). For Paul, the only difference between the Old Testament and the New Testament is that now God's people know how it is possible for God to give his righteousness to his people as a gift by faith. It is the death and resurrection of Jesus that makes it possible.

For the rest of Chapter 3 and all of Chapter 4, Paul makes a case for the purpose of the law codes in the Old Testament and discusses the relationship of the Old Testament to the Christian. Paul argues that the law codes were designed to lead God's people to faith in Christ. Before Jesus came to earth, the law served as a teacher, but now that Jesus has risen from the dead, God's people—Jewish people and gentiles together—have graduated from that teacher and are freed from the law (Galatians 3:23–4:7, 5:1).

In Galatians 5 and 6, Paul anticipates the inevitable question: "If the law codes in the Old Testament are not a description of righteousness and of how God wants us to live, then how do we know how to live to please God?" Paul ends his letter by explaining what it means to live righteously by living out the life of Christ. Paul calls this the "law of Christ" (Galatians 6:2) and follows up with numerous examples for the Christian to follow.

In order to live out the law of Christ, Christians must serve one another. Christians must not gratify the lusts of the flesh, and they should bear the "fruit of the Spirit" (Galatians 5:22–24). Christians should not be conceited or bent on provoking others, and Christians should try not to be a burden to others so they can help bear the burdens of those in need. Christians should be generous when it comes to taking care of their spiritual leaders and those in need.

KEY TAKEAWAYS

Paul concludes Galatians as aggressively as he begins. The Judaizers are obsessively concerned with marking their bodies (circumcision) as a sign that they are righteous before God. Paul, however, insists that it is his body that "bears the marks of the Lord Jesus" (Galatians 6:17). Just as Jesus' body was marked at his crucifixion so that he could bring salvation to the whole world, so the body of the missionary is marked with the scars of dangers and persecution to get the good news of Jesus to the whole world.

EPHESIANS

Living Like Christ

> "I therefore, the prisoner of the Lord, beseech you that ye walk
> worthy of the vocation wherewith ye are called."
> —Ephesians 4:1

Christians throughout the centuries have found Ephesians to be one of the loftiest presentations of the spiritual truths of Christianity. Ephesians puts on display the greatness of God's plan for this age and the age to come and then encourages the followers of Jesus to live lives that are worthy of God's grand plan.

A LETTER TO EPHESUS... AND BEYOND?

Ephesians, by its own accounting, is one of the letters that the Apostle Paul wrote to Christians living in and around the city of Ephesus, on the western coast of modern-day Turkey. The traditional view holds that Ephesians was written during Paul's first Roman imprisonment around A.D. 60, though there are many scholarly theories regarding the dating and authenticity of some of Paul's letters. Paul spent several years in Ephesus preaching and helping to plant Christian congregations in the city, which almost immediately engaged in missionary activity themselves.

The Temple of Artemis

The temple to the goddess Artemis (called Diana by the Romans and in the KJV) was located in ancient Ephesus and is one of the Seven Wonders of the Ancient World. When Paul visited Ephesus (Acts 19), a group of craftsmen who worshipped Artemis/Diana opposed Paul's preaching and incited a mob that chanted, "Great is Diana of the Ephesians."

Nearly all modern translations read something like, "To the saints which are at Ephesus, and to the faithful in Christ Jesus" in Ephesians 1:1, but a handful of ancient manuscripts omit the word "Ephesus." Some scholars argue that this was omitted by mistake, because the resulting sentence is choppy, and the manuscripts that omit these words still have the letter titled as "to the Ephesians." But many scholars believe that the original sentence in Ephesians 1 read something like "to the saints who are also being faithful in Christ Jesus," suggesting that perhaps the letter was originally designed to be circulated among a number of churches in that area and was not written just to the Ephesians.

THE LETTER'S OCCASION AND PURPOSE

Ephesians situates those who believe in Jesus right in the middle of God's great plan to make Jesus Christ the culmination of all things. Those who were the enemies of God are saved by being made into his children, and all powers, mortal and spiritual who oppose Jesus in the end will face the judgment of God. In Jesus, all Christians are unified into one body, the church. Paul then calls his readers to live out their "calling" as people who have experienced the power of Jesus in their lives.

While the purpose of Ephesians is abundantly clear, its occasion is not. Since Ephesians does not contain any of Paul's customary problem-solving, it is difficult to tell why he wrote these words to those people at that time. Most letters in the New Testament have an obvious inciting event that prompted their writing, but if Ephesians had such an inciting event, it is not obviously disclosed anywhere in the letter. Paul spent years living with the Ephesians, so the possibilities as to the occasion for the writing of Ephesians are many. The impersonal nature of the letter may be further evidence that the letter was designed to circulate among a large number of Christian congregations beyond Ephesus.

LIVING A HIGH CALLING

The flow of Ephesians follows Paul's normal pattern of presenting theological truths up front—such as truths about God, sin, Jesus, people, the gospel—and then using the second part of the letter to illustrate how someone who really believes these things lives life.

In Ephesians 1, Paul greets his audience, and then summarizes how God puts believers in Jesus at the center of his plan for this age and the age to come. Then Paul offers a powerful prayer of thanksgiving for what God has done among the Ephesians and in the world.

In Ephesians 2, Paul explains who the Ephesians were before they came to faith in Christ: "dead in trespasses and sins" (Ephesians 2:1) and followers (wittingly or unwittingly) of evil spiritual powers. There is surprisingly little in Paul's letters about Satan and demons, but they do appear to be what Paul has in mind when he uses the words "the prince of the power of the air" (Ephesians 2:2). Paul has already made clear to the Ephesians that Satan's defeat is certain, and he reassures the Ephesians that God is merciful, and through

Jesus Christ, is taking those people who had made themselves God's enemies, saving them, and then adopting them into His family.

Throughout Ephesians 3, Paul unveils for his readers the mystery of Christ. In the Old Testament, God promised that He would send a Savior who would provide salvation to people from every nation on earth. In Ephesians 3, Paul explains that now, in Christ, God has unveiled how He is doing just that. Jewish people and gentiles are in one body, the church of Jesus, and God is sending that church, through missionaries like Paul, into the world to proclaim the good news.

In Ephesians 4–6, Paul illustrates what it means to live a life that is worthy of God's great plan:

- Christians are to be unified in their mission because unity of purpose is a requirement for Christian spiritual growth.
- Christians are to think differently about the world and the people in it because they now see the world as God sees it. Paul firmly believes that people who think differently live differently.
- Christians are to walk in love, submitting themselves to one another.
- Christians are to live out the gospel in their marriages, in their parenting, and in their work.
- Christians are to adorn themselves with Christian virtue every day, like a Roman soldier suiting up in armor to go to war.

KEY TAKEAWAYS

In a remarkable way, Ephesians takes the profound truths of the Christian faith, explains them clearly, and then relates them to Paul's readers then and now. The good news about Jesus is not only God's grand plan for this age and the age to come; it is also an ethic by which to live life.

PHILIPPIANS

Paul's Celebration of the Philippians' Faith

"Stand fast in one spirit, with one mind striving together for the faith of the gospel."
—Philippians 1:27

Philippians is perhaps the most joyful of all of Paul's letters. Paul is clearly fond of the Philippians and is proud of their spiritual growth. Unlike many of Paul's earlier letters, Philippians offers little in the way of correction. The letter calls for the continued unity of the believers in Philippi in the faith and mission of Jesus. The letter is also a thank you for the ongoing financial and personnel support of the Philippians for Paul's mission.

A LETTER TO THE ROMAN COLONY OF PHILIPPI

The letter to the Philippians bears Paul's name, and it is believed to be from the hand of Paul even by the most critical and skeptical of scholars. Paul is clearly in prison in Rome when he writes (Philippians 1:12–13, 4:21). This would put the writing of Philippians sometime around A.D. 60.

The city of Philippi sits in the very north of Greece, an area called *Macedonia* in the New Testament (not to be confused with the modern country of Macedonia). The city of Philippi was turned into a Roman colony after the Battle of Philippi in 42 B.C. The city quickly grew in wealth, and during Paul's day, its citizens were proud of their status as a Roman colony. Paul arrived in Philippi on his second missionary journey (probably around A.D. 50). This was Paul's first missionary trip to Europe (see Acts 16). After Paul preached in Philippi, a number of Philippians became followers of Jesus, and the Philippian Christians became some of Paul's greatest supporters.

THE MOST FAMOUS THANK-YOU LETTER IN HISTORY

When the Philippians discovered that Paul was in prison in Rome, they sent a member of their congregation, Epaphroditus, to Rome with financial support to help the mission continue. During that trip, Epaphroditus became very ill and almost died. The occasion for the writing of Philippians, consequently, is to update the Philippians on Paul's arrest and imprisonment, report to them on how Epaphroditus is doing after his illness, and to thank them for the financial support they provided.

In the letter, Paul encourages the Philippians to continue being unified in Christ's mission, and Paul offers them three examples to follow. Paul also warns the Philippians about the dangers of false teachers, and he encourages them to set their minds on Christian virtue.

A LIFE WORTHY OF THE GOSPEL

In Philippians 1, Paul prays for the Philippians and updates them on his circumstances. Paul is confident that he will get out of prison and continue his mission, but he instructs the Philippians that the

Christian does not have to be afraid of death. "To live is Christ," he says, "and to die is gain" (Philippians 1:21). In life, Paul has the great privilege of serving Christ, and in death, he will go home to be with Christ, which he believes is a great reward. For Paul, this is a win-win situation. Since no one knows when or how they will die, Christians should always live lives that are worthy of the gospel.

In Philippians 2, Paul encourages the Philippians to stay unified in their faith and in their mission. Paul gives the Philippians three examples of this kind of thinking: Jesus, Timothy, and Epaphroditus. Jesus was willing to set aside everything, including all the glories of heaven, to come to earth to provide salvation for all people. If he was willing to do that, then Christians should be willing to take that good news of salvation to the ends of the earth. This is what Timothy has done. No one cares more about people than Timothy, and Epaphroditus was willing to risk his life for the sake of the gospel. These are the kinds of people that Christians should honor and emulate.

An Ancient Hymn?

Because of the rhythmic, almost lyrical language in Philippians 2:6–11, Paul may be quoting an ancient Christian hymn or poem. If true, this text provides a window into what the earliest Christians believed about Jesus perhaps decades before Paul; namely, that Jesus was God come to earth in human form.

In Philippians 3, Paul warns the Philippians about the dangers of false teachers and reminds them of his own testimony. Paul's past is filled with regrets. But he has the strength to press on with joy because Christ has made him a part of God's family. Paul is not afraid of his past sins because he has received the righteousness of

God that comes from faith in Jesus, a righteousness that replaces his own faults. Paul, a Roman citizen himself, concludes the chapter with an admonition to the Philippians that their citizenship is not ultimately in Rome but in heaven. Their most important allegiance is not to their own country but to the Kingdom of God.

Paul closes out the letter in Philippians 4 with a kind thank you for all the help the Philippians have provided to him. He encourages them to focus their minds on Christian virtue and then reminds them that God cares for His children. God used the Philippians to care for Paul, and if the Philippians are ever in need, God will likewise care for them.

KEY TAKEAWAYS

Paul uses the words *joy* and *rejoice* more than a dozen times in Philippians. He rejoices in their unity in the gospel. He rejoices in all the help they sent him on his travels and while in prison in Rome. And he rejoices that God has given His people such excellent examples to follow, especially the example of Christ.

COLOSSIANS

An Early Record of Christian Thinking about Ancient
Religions and Philosophies

"As ye have therefore received Christ Jesus the Lord, so walk ye in him: Rooted
and built up in him, and stablished in the faith, as ye have been taught."
—Colossians 2:6–7

Colossians features one of the earliest records of Christian thinking about the philosophies and religions of the ancient world. Many
of these religious beliefs are unrecognizable to modern readers
because those religions, by and large, no longer exist. Colossians
provides not just a historical glimpse into ancient Christian thinking; it provides a model for Christian thinking that has endured
throughout the centuries.

A LETTER TO THE LYCUS RIVER VALLEY

The text of Colossians identifies itself as a letter from the Apostle
Paul to Christians living in the city of Colossae in the Lycus River
Valley in Asia Minor (Turkey). Scholars have traditionally believed
that Colossians was written during Paul's first Roman imprisonment,
around A.D. 60. As with Ephesians, there are many scholarly theories
regarding its dating and authenticity, but even a number of critical
and secular scholars advocate for this traditional view.

Colossae's Earthquake

The city of Colossae was wrecked by an earthquake around A.D. 60, and the area never truly recovered. This has led many scholars to suggest an early date for Colossians, a date before the earthquake. The city was all but abandoned by A.D. 400, and the site has never been excavated.

Asia Minor was a hotbed of religious diversity and ingenuity in the ancient world. It is no wonder that Paul writes to the Christians there to help them think "Christianly" about all the big ideas of their day. Colossians mentions a number of false teachings that were prevalent in Colossae in Paul's day: Greek philosophy, mysticism, asceticism, the mystery religions, and esoteric religious practices. Many of these ideas were deeply rooted in the philosophical and theological milieu that gave birth to second-century Gnosticism—an ancient worldview that held as a central belief the notion that the spiritual world is good and the physical world is evil.

Identifying a single group of false teachers inside the church who promoted these ideas (like the Judaizers described in Acts and Galatians) is impossible, and it does not appear that is what the letter is about. Paul's letter to the Galatians provides a clear picture of what it looks like when Paul attacks false teachers in the churches, and Colossians is very unlike Galatians. Rather, Paul is warning the Christians in Colossae that if they do not think carefully about the ideas in the culture around them, they will be "spoiled" (Colossians 2:8) or taken captive in the metaphorical sense by these ideas and not stay true to the Christian faith.

A HANDBOOK FOR CHRISTIAN THINKING

Paul writes as though he has never been to the city of Colossae. A man named Epaphras from the city of Colossae, who probably connected with Paul during the years that Paul was in Ephesus, brought the gospel to Colossae. Now that Paul is in prison, he is writing to the Christian congregations in Colossae to check on them and model for them Christian thinking on the various philosophical and religious traditions present in Asia Minor. Paul's tone in Colossians is instructive, but he does appear worried about these Christians because he's never been there himself to teach them.

Paul's model for Christian thinking is straightforward and intuitive. For Paul, step one requires Christians to understand the truths about Jesus and Jesus' teaching. Step two requires them to apply those truths to any ideas that come their way. Step three requires them to live out those truths in every aspect of life.

FROM IDEA TO ETHICS

In Colossians 1, Paul greets his audience and offers a prayer of gratitude for all that God has done among the Colossians. He is particularly thankful for the missionaries who brought the gospel to Colossae. Paul then transitions to his deeply theological presentation of Christ. Christ is the creator. He is God made visible, and in him dwells all the fullness of God. He is the Lord of all things and he is the Savior of the world.

Colossians 2 records Paul's critiques of some of the philosophies and religious beliefs of his day. He takes the truths of Christ presented in Chapter 1 and applies them to those ideas in Chapter 2. Paul argues, for example, that when Christians understand that in

Christ dwells all the fullness of God (the Greek word *pleroma*), they will not be duped by religious notions that locate the fullness of God outside of Jesus and make Jesus some lesser being than God. Paul also argues that ascetic practices—the rigorous denial of bodily desires—have no power to fix what is spiritually wrong with a person: Only the gospel can do that. Paul does teach, in other places, ascetic-like practices (fasting, abstinence from sex for a spiritual purpose, etc.), but here he is clear that, while those may be aids in spiritual focus, they are of no value in stopping fleshly indulgences.

Paul moves from the theological to the practical in Chapters 3 and 4. For Paul, ideas always lead to ethics. In a fashion very similar to Ephesians, Paul calls Christians to set their minds on heavenly things and to "put on" Christian virtue like a garment. Likewise, Christians are to "put off" and "mortify" ("put to death," metaphorically) sinful habits and desires (Colossians 3:1–17). Paul then reminds the Colossians that Christians are to live out the gospel in their marriages, their parenting, and their work. Most of the rest of Chapter 4 is concerned with Paul's plans and introducing other Christian missionaries to the Colossian congregations.

KEY TAKEAWAYS

Colossians served as a handbook for Christian thinking in the ancient church and still serves that purpose two thousand years later. Though many of the ideas Paul examines feel long gone in the twenty-first century, Colossians is still incredibly relevant to modern Christian thinking. Christian thinking must always begin with the truth about Jesus Christ and his gospel and examine everything in light of that truth.

1-2 THESSALONIANS

Paul's Concern for the Believers in Thessalonica

> "We were comforted over you in all our affliction and distress by your faith:
> For now we live, if ye stand fast in the Lord."
> —1 Thessalonians 3:7–8

These two short letters to the new Christians in the city of Thessalonica capture Paul's deep concern for the people he meets on his missionary journeys. Paul writes the Thessalonians two letters to finish some of his teaching, answer their questions, and prepare them for the suffering and persecution that are likely to continue now that they are Christians.

THE GOSPEL GOES TO EUROPE

Paul first visited the city of Thessalonica in northern Greece on his second missionary journey around A.D. 50. Acts 17 tells the story of his stay there. After Paul spends some time preaching in Thessalonica, a large number of Thessalonians convert to Christianity. These conversions create quite a stir in the city. Eventually, a mob forms and begins dragging Christians out of their homes. Paul has to flee the city by night and travels south.

By the time Paul lands in the city of Corinth, he is worried about what happened in Thessalonica after he left, so he sends Timothy, his disciple, to check on the Christians there (1 Thessalonians 2:17–3:5). After hearing about their state from Timothy and likely receiving questions from Timothy, Paul writes 1 Thessalonians. Timothy carries the letter to the Thessalonians and returns with more questions, sparking Paul to write 2 Thessalonians, probably just a few months later.

Ancient Thessalonica

Thessalonica was almost four hundred years old when Paul preached there. The city was founded by Cassander of Macedon and named after Alexander the Great's sister. Thessaloniki (as it is known today) survived conquests, massacres, and wars, and is currently one of the most visited tourist places in Greece.

QUESTIONS FROM THE THESSALONIANS

Both 1 and 2 Thessalonians deal with several concerns, one of which was accusations being made about the missionaries by the angry citizens of Thessalonica. Many of them concern money. It is likely that the Christian missionaries were being accused of preaching this new religion in order to bilk people out of their money. Paul reminds the Thessalonians that his message there was spiritual and not about money, and that when the missionaries ran out of money, they did not ask the Thessalonians for financial support; they got jobs so as not to burden the new Christians. Paul also spends some time in both letters dealing with issues of morality: sexual morality, brotherly love, and a strong work ethic.

Perhaps some of the most interesting and surprising material in 1 and 2 Thessalonians, however, concerns the questions the Thessalonian Christians have for Paul about suffering in this life and how that connects to the end of the world. Paul, no doubt, taught them what Jesus himself taught about the end of the world and the Kingdom of

God, and this, along with perhaps Paul's sudden departure from the city and their own suffering, sparked a number of questions from them.

THE LETTERS IN BRIEF

In 1 Thessalonians 1–2, Paul greets the Thessalonian Christians and invites them to remember how the missionaries behaved when they were in the city—they acted in a godly manner, taught the Thessalonians the Scripture, and never asked them for money. Paul concludes Chapter 2 by thanking God for the Thessalonians, because they believed the word of God and became genuine followers of Jesus.

In 1 Thessalonians 3, Paul explains why he has not been back to Thessalonica to check on them himself. Paul is now a lightning rod of conflict in northern Greece, so he sends Timothy in his place. Paul discusses the good report he received from Timothy about the Thessalonian Christians—they are living faithfully even in difficult times.

Paul begins 1 Thessalonians 4 by reiterating the teaching of Jesus on sexual purity, and then throughout Chapters 4 and 5, Paul answers some basic questions the Thessalonians have about the end of the world. Jesus himself taught that he would one day return (as discussed in Matthew 24). Paul, no doubt, taught this to the Thessalonians. But they were apparently worried that if someone died before Jesus returned, they would miss out on the resurrection on the last day. Paul reassures them that all those who believe in Jesus, living or dead, will live eternally in the resurrection. Paul, following the example of Jesus, is quick to remind the Thessalonians that no one knows when these things will happen.

By the opening of 2 Thessalonians 1, it is clear that the Thessalonians are now suffering persecution. Paul reassures them that even though it may seem as though God is oblivious to their suffering and that evil is winning, they should take the long view. Even if the righteous never get any relief in this life, and even if the wicked go to their graves without having been punished for their evil deeds, one day Jesus will return, and he will rescue the righteous and judge the wicked.

In Chapter 2, Paul returns to answering questions about the return of Jesus. Is it possible that Jesus could return and his followers not know? Paul describes several of the wild and mysterious events that will happen in the last days such as the appearing of the "man of lawlessness" whose coming is "after the working of Satan with all power and signs and lying wonders" (2 Thessalonians 2:9) as a way of reassuring the Thessalonians that when Jesus returns, no one will wonder if it has happened.

Paul concludes 2 Thessalonians by encouraging believers to be faithful and work hard to take care of one another. He warns that some people will claim to follow Jesus but live in open defiance against his teaching. "Have no company with him, that he may be ashamed," Paul says. This, however, is instructive and not punitive. "Yet count him not as an enemy, but admonish him as a brother" (2 Thessalonians 3:14–15).

KEY TAKEAWAYS

Paul's concern for the believers in Thessalonica takes center stage in 1 and 2 Thessalonians. He is concerned for their well-being in the midst of persecution, and he is concerned that they get their questions answered—questions about Christian doctrine and questions about Christian living. Most importantly, Paul reminds these Christians that one day Jesus will return to rescue the suffering and to bring God's kingdom to earth.

1–2 TIMOTHY AND TITUS

The Pastoral Letters

"And the things that thou hast heard of me among many witnesses, the same commit thou to faithful men, who shall be able to teach others also."
—2 Timothy 2:2

1-2 Timothy and Titus are often referred to as the *Pastoral Letters* because they address many questions related to the everyday work of the pastoral ministry, the spiritual leadership over a local congregation. As Paul contemplates heading to Spain on what would be his final mission trip, he wants to pass the torch of leadership to his disciples, Timothy and Titus.

LETTERS AT THE END OF PAUL'S LIFE

Both 1-2 Timothy and Titus are among those letters of Paul that are most questioned by modern critical scholars as to their authenticity. Nevertheless, such arguments are relatively recent in the history of Christianity, and the earliest Christians both reference the letters and cite them as being written by Paul.

Both 1 Timothy and Titus purport to be written while Paul is out of prison and traveling in the eastern Mediterranean. Most likely, then, Paul is setting up Titus in Crete and Timothy in the city of Ephesus in preparation for his fourth missionary journey to Spain around A.D. 65. Paul identifies that he is in Macedonia (northern Greece) when he writes 1 Timothy but gives no mention of his location in Titus.

In 2 Timothy, Paul is back in prison, most likely in Rome, and he knows that his death is near (e.g., 2 Timothy 4:6). He writes his final words of encouragement to Timothy, probably around A.D. 67, and is martyred shortly after.

Why Was Paul Executed?

It is not clear what charges led to Paul's execution, but it is likely that he fell victim to Emperor Nero's mass persecution of Christians following a devastating fire in Rome (A.D. 64) for which Christians may have been blamed. According to the earliest Christians, Paul was beheaded.

PAUL PREPARES THE CHURCHES FOR HIS FINAL JOURNEY

1 Timothy and Titus were written to prepare Timothy and Titus to take over for Paul as leaders among the Christians while Paul takes the mission to Spain. These two letters are similar in places, due primarily to their similar purposes, so it is helpful to look at their content together.

In 1 Timothy 1 and Titus 1, Paul warns about the dangers of false teachers. Paul expects that more and more errors will crop up in the churches, and he instructs Timothy and Titus that it is the job of the Christian leader to teach, exhort, and even rebuke, when necessary, those who are teaching things contrary to what Jesus taught.

Prayer is the focus of 1 Timothy 2. Paul wants Timothy to teach Christians to pray for a government that will leave them alone to accomplish the mission. Paul expects that a devout prayer life will be a great aid in holiness, peacefulness, and unity (e.g., 1 Timothy 2:8).

In 1 Timothy 3 and Titus 1, Paul gives qualifications for pastors or elders. The pastor must have a demonstrable history of faithfulness—faithfulness in service, leadership, and family. The qualified pastor does not have a history of philandering, drunkenness, or greed, and this person has an honorable reputation with non-Christians in the community.

Teaching sound doctrine is the focus of 1 Timothy 4–5 and Titus 2. Paul expects this will be a difficult task in the days ahead. In addition, it is not only the duty of the pastor to teach sound doctrine; it is also the job of older, more mature Christians to teach younger Christians. For Paul, sound doctrine is not just the lofty theological truths of the Christian faith. Sound doctrine includes how to be a good husband or wife, mother or father, boss or employee.

Paul concludes 1 Timothy and Titus with an admonition to be a good neighbor, and someone who, as much as is possible, obeys the laws, tries to get along with everyone, and lives righteously. Both letters end with a gospel reminder from Paul: Being a good person is not what makes one a Christian. Salvation is through the mercy of God by faith in Jesus. Paul says, "Not by works of righteousness which we have done, but according to his mercy he saved us" (Titus 3:5). Paul, however, is convinced that those who follow Jesus will live like Jesus lived, and this will result in all sorts of good works in the world. Christians proclaim the truth of the gospel and show the world how much God loves them by doing good works.

PAUL'S LAST WORDS

In many ways, 2 Timothy serves as Paul's final words to one of his closest friends and, by extension, to the whole Christian church. In 2 Timothy 1, Paul reminds Timothy to remain faithful to Christ and his mission even when the people around him are being unfaithful.

Paul uses three analogies in 2 Timothy 2 to remind Timothy about the challenges and rewards of remaining faithful to Christ. Paul encourages Timothy to:

- Remain as focused as a soldier who is about to be deployed
- Live a life of integrity like a winning athlete who does not break the rules
- Work as hard at serving Christ as a farmer works to feed himself

Throughout 2 Timothy 2–4, Paul is convinced that Timothy will only be able to remain faithful if he continues being a student of the Scripture and if he stays disciplined in his life to "flee also youthful lusts" (2 Timothy 2:22). Paul exhorts Timothy to stay the course in what he has learned from Paul, even though the world will be filled with those who are unfaithful, and Paul exhorts Timothy to faithfully "preach the word" (2 Timothy 4:2).

Paul concludes 2 Timothy with a reminder of God's faithfulness. Over and over again, God rescued Paul from danger as he accomplished the mission that God had for him. "I was delivered out of the mouth of the lion," Paul says, and he believes that God is going to rescue him one more time, but this time into his "heavenly kingdom" (2 Timothy 4:17–18).

KEY TAKEAWAYS

The Pastoral Letters are filled with practical advice about how to live a faithful life of leadership and service. They contain specific instructions for pastors and spiritual leaders. They also record the final words of the Apostle Paul and stand as a clear exposition of the Christian view of a life well lived for the mission of God.

PHILEMON

A Christian Condemnation of Slavery

"If thou count me therefore a partner, receive [Onesimus] as myself."
—Philemon 17

Philemon is the shortest and perhaps the most personal of Paul's letters. The letter has received little scholarly scrutiny compared to Paul's other letters, but Philemon is a shining example of Paul's brilliant use of language to persuade. Philemon also clearly demonstrates Paul's ethical thinking and stands as a crystal-clear repudiation of slavery in Christian thought.

A LETTER ABOUT AN ENSLAVED PERSON

Scholars generally agree that Philemon was written by Paul, while he was in prison, most likely in Rome. Paul's letter to Philemon is connected to his letter to the Colossians, so it could be slightly earlier, perhaps in the late A.D. 50s, but not later than A.D. 62.

The letter is addressed to Philemon, an acquaintance of Paul, and is about an enslaved person named Onesimus who escaped his enslaver, became a Christian, and now wants to gain his freedom. Since two of the people mentioned in Philemon, Onesimus and Archippus, are also named in Paul's letter to the Colossians, it is probable that Philemon also lived in Colossae and thus was the destination of the letter to him. It is also likely that when Paul writes "receive him" (Philemon 17) with regard to Onesimus, he indicates that Onesimus himself is the one delivering the letter to Philemon.

THE STORY OF ONESIMUS

Trying to reconstruct a historical event from reading a single letter is an imperfect endeavor, but a careful reading of Philemon yields the following as the most likely scenario.

Philemon is a relatively wealthy man who enslaved at least one person. When Philemon becomes a Christian, his faith does not immediately change the way he thinks about his economy or his enslaved people. At some point, a man named Onesimus escapes from his enslaver, Philemon, probably robbing him in the process in order to have the money to escape. Onesimus lands in Rome and meets Paul while Paul is still in prison. Onesimus subsequently becomes a Christian and begins serving with Paul in the mission there in Rome. Eventually, Paul learns that Onesimus is still legally enslaved to Philemon, a man Paul knows. Paul writes the letter to Philemon and asks Onesimus to deliver it. The general intention of the letter is to change Philemon's thinking on the subject of slavery, and the specific intention is to get Philemon to release Onesimus from slavery and send him back to Rome so Onesimus can continue serving in the mission there.

Slavery in the Roman World

Scholars estimate that one out of every three people in Rome in Paul's day were enslaved. People became enslaved for a variety of reasons (because they owed money, were criminals, had been captured as military prisoners, etc.) and were from all over the European and Mediterranean worlds. It was illegal throughout the Roman Empire to harbor an enslaved person who had escaped their enslaver.

A CHRISTIAN THINKS ABOUT SLAVERY

Philemon has never been divided into chapters due to its short length and therefore it is probably best to think of the argument of the letter rather than its outline.

Paul begins his argument on the issue of slavery with a declaration of what is right. Paul is very bold in Christ to command Philemon to do what is right. There is no question in Paul's mind what the right thing is for a Christian enslaver to do—free his enslaved people! But Paul would rather persuade than command. He continues, "Yet for love's sake I rather beseech thee" (Philemon 9). Paul wants to change Philemon's mind.

Paul then appeals to the fact that he is in prison for the gospel, probably intended as a humorous reference—"Surely you will not disappoint the old man, and did I mention I am in jail?" Paul calls Onesimus his child and his very heart. If Paul can change Philemon's thinking about the person, he can change his thinking about slavery. Paul intimates that Onesimus's escape from slavery was a part of God's plan, and Paul pleads with Philemon to treat Onesimus just as he would treat Paul. No Christian would dare to own Paul the Apostle, so how then is it right to own some other person?

Paul then makes a fourfold argument to persuade Philemon to release Onesimus and return him to the ministry in Rome:

1. First, Paul repeatedly mentions how useful Onesimus is to the ministry in Rome (e.g., Philemon 13).
2. Second, it was common for Christians to support missionaries by giving them money so they could travel to their destination. Paul suggests that Philemon should begin thinking of whatever financial loss he might suffer as a result of freeing Onesimus and forgiving his theft in this way.

3. Third, Paul offers to repay any of the financial damage Onesimus's escape might have caused, though Paul quickly points out the absurdity of such an offer considering what Philemon owes the missionaries—"Albeit I do not say to thee how thou owest unto me even thine own self besides" (Philemon 19).

4. Fourth, Paul says that he is sure that he will be free from prison soon and plans to stay with Philemon the next time he passes through Asia Minor. That is how confident he is that Philemon will do the right thing.

Paul regularly addresses himself to enslaved people in his letters. He encourages them to obtain their freedom if they can (e.g., 1 Corinthians 7:21) but gives them direct instructions for how to live as followers of Jesus even if they cannot. Modern readers often misread this posture toward the enslaved person as Paul being "soft" on the issue of slavery. It is much more likely that Paul feels compelled to help them live the Christian life because they were so numerous in the Roman Empire, and the opportunity for freedom was rare.

KEY TAKEAWAYS

Though only a handful of paragraphs, Philemon contains some really important ideas. Paul never addresses the governmental institution of slavery, but he paints slavery as entirely unchristian and destroys any distinction of status in the church between the enslaved person and the enslaver. The Christians who have been at work throughout history to end slavery, from the ancient Roman Empire to the modern Civil Rights Movement, have found in Philemon a clear condemnation of slavery.

HEBREWS

Faithfulness to Christ Is Better Than Avoiding Persecution

"Let us run with patience the race that is set before us,
looking unto Jesus the author and finisher of our faith."
—Hebrews 12:1–2

The book of Hebrews was written to a group of Jewish Christians, who, under threat of persecution, were contemplating abandoning the faith and returning to Judaism. The author writes to warn them that their unfaithfulness is a far greater danger than persecution and to remind them that knowing Jesus is a far better reward than living a suffering-free life.

A PLEA FOR FAITHFULNESS TO JEWISH CHRISTIANS IN ROME

The book of Hebrews is technically anonymous, but the author appears to know his audience, and they know him. The author uses masculine endings to refer to himself (e.g., the Greek participle in Hebrews 11:32), and he writes in a way that leads many scholars to believe he had a Jewish upbringing. For most of history, Paul has been frequently named as the author of Hebrews, but even some ancient Christians express their doubt as to Pauline authorship. Modern scholars have a number of theories as to the authorship of Hebrews, and virtually all of them conclude that it was not Paul. Evidence in the text suggests that Hebrews was written after the

Christian mission to the gentiles was well underway and after a size-able population of Jewish Christians developed in Rome. It is also likely, given the way the author discusses the Jewish temple, that Hebrews was written before its destruction in A.D. 70. A date in the A.D. 60s, then, is perhaps the most reasonable.

The letter to the Hebrews was written to Jewish Christians, probably in Rome, who were beginning to suffer persecution for their faith. They were in danger of falling away from the faith (e.g., Hebrews 2:1, 6:6), so the author makes a plea for them to remain faithful to Jesus and to what they have been taught.

COMPARING JESUS TO THE GREAT FEATURES OF THE OLD TESTAMENT

To illustrate the reasonableness of faithfulness to Jesus, even in the midst of suffering, the author favorably compares Jesus to the classical features of the Old Testament that his Jewish Christian readers would hold very dear.

In Hebrews 1–2, the author compares Jesus with the angels of the Old Testament. Angels are "ministering spirits" (Hebrews 1:14), but Jesus is the Son of God. He is worshipped because he is God in a human body. Jesus is the creator, and he is eternal. The author of Hebrews concludes his comparison with a warning. When angels in the Old Testament brought a message from God and people disobeyed it, those people fell under terrible judgment. How much more peril should people expect to face if they disobey the message of Jesus who is God incarnate?

The author of Hebrews then moves to comparing Jesus to Moses and Joshua in Hebrews 3–4. Moses was God's servant who delivered

God's people out of slavery, and Joshua gave God's people a taste of rest in the promised land. Jesus is even greater than Moses and Joshua, because he is the creator. Jesus offers the ultimate, spiritual rest, something Joshua from the Old Testament could never give. The author warns his readers not to make the same mistake that the people of Israel made when they heard God's word and rejected it. That whole generation died in the wilderness. Why would these Jewish Christians in Rome think they would fare any differently if they disobeyed?

In Hebrews 4–10, the author compares Jesus to the Old Testament sacrificial system. The author argues that the priesthood, the tabernacle and the temple, the animal sacrifices, and the feast days were all signs of God's mercy and love. They were pictures of how God planned to deal with human sinfulness and offer His forgiveness. But those animal sacrifices could never fix what is wrong with people. The author argues, "For it is not possible that the blood of bulls and of goats should take away sins" (Hebrews 10:4). Each of those features of the Old Testament religious system were instructive pictures to teach God's people about God's Messiah. But Jesus offers even more than those features did:

- Jesus is a better priest than the Old Testament priesthood because he is perfect and he lives forever.
- Jesus is better than the old covenantal system because Jesus accomplishes what it could not: actual forgiveness of sins and a changed heart.
- Jesus is a better sacrifice than animal sacrifices because he, once and for all, took away sins.

To abandon following Christ to return to Judaism, even if only in practice to avoid persecution, makes little sense in light of who Jesus is and what he did.

Did Christians Believe That Jesus Was God?

The author of Hebrews, with the rest of the New Testament, depicts angels as worshipping Jesus, something a writer with a Jewish upbringing would never say if he did not believe that Jesus was God incarnate. The author also depicts God the Father speaking to Jesus and calling him God in Hebrews 1:8.

Hebrews 11–13 concludes the book with practical application. How does someone who genuinely believes Hebrews 1–10 live life? The author begins by taking a swift survey through the Old Testament to show how all the great "heroes of the faith" lived lives of faith, even though the promises of God's Messiah were still very far off from their perspective. Those people knew very little and still faithfully followed God. Jesus' followers should be even more faithful, since they live in light of the knowledge of Jesus' crucifixion and resurrection. Christians who genuinely believe in Jesus love others, show hospitality, take care of those in trouble, honor their marriages and stay sexually pure, do not love money, keep watch over one another, and pray.

KEY TAKEAWAYS

The author of Hebrews concludes this book where he started, with a declaration that faithfulness to Jesus is better than everything, even avoiding persecution. He writes that Jesus is "that great shepherd of the sheep" (Hebrews 13:20) who can "make you perfect in every good work to do his will" (Hebrews 13:21). It is a call to remain faithful to Jesus regardless of difficulties or dangers.

JAMES

Exhortations about Godly Living

> "But be ye doers of the word, and not hearers only, deceiving your own selves."
> —James 1:22

James might be one of the earliest Christian writings. It was written to Jewish Christians in a time before the faith had taken root among non-Jewish people. The letter is a series of exhortations, or sermons, to followers of Jesus. James contains exhortations about justice, exhortations about care for those in need, and, above all, exhortations about obedience to the Scripture.

A LETTER OF JAMES, BUT WHICH JAMES?

For most of the history of the Christian church, Christians have believed that James the Just, the brother of Jesus, wrote this letter. Today, though, there are many varied theories among scholars as to authorship. The letter identifies itself as being from James (written in the Greek as *Iakobos* or Jacob), "a servant of God and of the Lord Jesus Christ" (James 1:1).

Jacob or James?

The spelling of the name *Jacob* has changed as the Bible has been translated across the centuries from Hebrew to Greek to Latin to English. The Hebrew spelling, *Jacob*, is preserved in the Old Testament, and the Hellenized and Anglicized spelling, *James*, is often used in the New Testament.

Since dating the letter depends heavily on the identification of its author, modern scholars also have developed a wide variety of dates for James, though there is ample evidence as to its antiquity. James uses the Greek word for *synagogue* to describe the weekly gathering place of the Christians. He does not appear to be familiar with the texts of the Gospels, and he does not seem to have a notion of Christians who are not Jewish people. All of these point to an early date.

A COLLECTION OF SERMONS

The loose structure of James has produced many attempts to outline its contents. At its simplest, James is a letter that serves as a collection of exhortations to Christians about godly living. The author begins exhortations with "My brethren" followed by an imperative (James 1:2, 2:1, 3:1). The author also makes extensive use of rhetorical questions to move from exhortation to exhortation (e.g., 3:13, 4:1).

James typically begins each exhortation with a particular instruction, then argues the general principle, and then concludes with a specific example. A careful study of James reveals a number of consistent themes: maturity, righteousness, godly speech, divine wisdom, right attitude, and patience.

THE EXHORTATIONS OF JAMES

James begins his first exhortation, an exhortation to Christian maturity with the reassurance that, although God does not cause evil to befall His people, God does grow His people to maturity through difficult times. James then moves to a more general discussion of obedience to the Scripture as the key to spiritual maturity. A person who hears the Scripture but does not follow it is deceiving himself into thinking that he is following God. But the person who hears the Scripture and lives it "shall be blessed in his deed" (James 1:25). James concludes with some specific examples of obedience: self-control when it comes to speech and special care for the most vulnerable in society.

James's second exhortation on righteousness begins with a warning about showing favoritism, especially as it relates to wealth and class. Christians should live lives of justice and mercy. The person who claims to have faith in Jesus but does not perform "good works" does not live out the life of God as God instructs. That person has a dead faith, which is no faith at all. James illustrates this principle with some specific examples of people from the Old Testament who clearly had genuine faith in God and demonstrated it by the way they lived.

Earliest Christian Practice

The very first Christians were culturally Jewish, and many of them remained so throughout their lives. They continued to attend the synagogue and preached Jesus' teachings in the temple in Jerusalem (e.g., Acts 3). Even Paul the Apostle continued many Torah practices throughout his life.

Most of James 3 is an exhortation about the tongue. The words people say, James argues, can be used to teach people about God, but words can also be used to destroy people. The way a person speaks can turn an entire life around, for good or for evil, and the person who can control the tongue is rare indeed. Often, out of the same mouth comes praise for God and the cursing of others. "My brethren, these things ought not so to be" (James 3:10). The way a person speaks reveals their true heart. James concludes this exhortation with a reminder about wisdom. Evil wisdom, just like evil speaking, is not what God wants for his people, and godly wisdom is easy to identify. Godly wisdom leads people to be "peaceable, gentle, and easy to be intreated, full of mercy and good fruits, without partiality, and without hypocrisy" (James 3:17).

The exhortation in James 4 concerns attitude. James argues that selfishness, covetousness, and belligerence produce strife and hatred among believers in Jesus. James calls this behavior spiritual adultery and says that Christians who have this sort of attitude oppose God. The remedy for this attitude is humility, submission to God, repentance, and trust in God's mercy. James concludes his exhortation with specific examples of a godly attitude. A godly attitude is one that is not judgmental. It is an attitude of humility about the future and a proper understanding about wealth and people in need. This last example contains some of the strongest language anywhere in James. God hears the cries of those who have been exploited by the wicked rich, and those who do the exploiting will face the judgment of God.

KEY TAKEAWAYS

James concludes his letter with an exhortation that encompasses all the others. It is an exhortation to patience, but not patience in the general sense. It refers to how Christians are patiently waiting for the return of the Lord. And while Christians wait, they endure hardship. Through it all, they keep their word, and they take care of those who are sick and spiritually weak. Christians pray, and they hold one another accountable for living a life of godliness.

1 PETER

Peter's Thoughts on Suffering

"But and if ye suffer for righteousness' sake, happy are ye:
and be not afraid of their terror, neither be troubled."
—1 Peter 3:14

The letter called 1 Peter is one of the most comprehensive discussions of suffering in the New Testament. While it is not the only place in the Bible that suffering appears, 1 Peter stands as a powerful call to the Christian to endure suffering well as a righteous testimony to Jesus and the gospel.

PETER'S FIRST LETTER

Though contemporary scholarship has many theories as to the composition and date of 1 Peter, it is traditionally believed to be written by Peter the Apostle, near the end of Peter's life in the A.D. 60s. The letter names the audience: Christians in the Roman provinces of Asia Minor (Turkey).

The letter of 1 Peter is primarily about suffering, especially the kind of suffering that is brought on by others. While it is true that during the lifetime of Peter the Apostle, Rome had no empire-wide policy of persecuting Christians, it is also true that local persecution under the direction of Nero certainly happened in Rome. And there are many forms of "suffering" that can be brought upon a religious minority that, while terrible in their effect, fall short of official governmental persecution. The author likely has both of these situations in mind as he writes.

Peter's Name

Peter the Apostle was born *Simon*. Jesus gave him the nickname "rock," *Petros* in Greek, from which translations get the name *Peter*. In Aramaic, however, the nickname is *Cephas*. Both versions of Peter's nickname appear in the New Testament, though *Peter* is far more common.

CHRISTIANITY AND SUFFERING

Peter begins his letter by greeting his audience and pronouncing a blessing of God over them. He acknowledges that they are suffering through a difficult time and encourages them to continue to love God and to wait for God's rescue. The chapter ends with an encouragement for Christians to live out the gospel—be ready, be vigilant, and "hope to the end for the grace that is to be brought unto you at the revelation of Jesus Christ" (1 Peter 1:13).

Patience, Even in Exile

Christians can expect God to deliver them from suffering and persecution, but that rescue may not come in this life. Christians are waiting for Jesus to return as he said he would, and it is then that they will receive their true rescue, "an inheritance incorruptible, and undefiled" that does not fade away, "reserved in heaven for you" (1 Peter 1:4). That is why, regardless of the circumstances, the Christian faith and hope should live in God.

In 1 Peter 2–3, Peter continues a theme he introduced in Chapter 1. Christians should think of their time in this world in the same way that the people of Israel thought about their time in captivity in Babylon. In Chapter 1, Peter calls his audience elect exiles, and in Chapter 2, he uses many of the terms the Old Testament uses to describe God's people in Israel to describe these non-Jewish believers. He calls them "a chosen generation, a royal priesthood, an holy nation, a peculiar people" (1 Peter 2:9). Followers of Jesus are in this world just as the ancient Israelites were in Babylon, but this "exile" is temporary. Just as the people of Israel returned to their home, so Christians will leave this world and return to their true home.

Everyday Life

Because this world is not their true home, Christians live differently than the gentiles (non-believers) do. Christians are to lay aside all malice, deception, hypocrisy, and evil speaking. Christians are to live among their neighbors with the utmost integrity. Christians are to, as best they can, obey the government, be good citizens, and be respectful to those in authority over them. Christians are to live out the gospel within their families (1 Peter 3:1–7). Peter wants his audience to live in such a way that when suffering and persecution come, there will be no doubt in anyone's mind why the Christians are suffering. They are suffering for their faith, and their suffering is not deserved.

Peter concludes Chapters 2 and 3 with reminders of the gospel. Jesus was both just and innocent, and yet he suffered at the hands of evil people so that God might save evil people from their sins. Likewise, the Christian should never be surprised when suffering comes. Christians follow in Christ's footsteps, even into suffering. It is the Christian calling.

In 1 Peter 4, Peter continues to explain how both suffering and the knowledge that one day Jesus will return leads Christians to godly living. Suffering puts the world in its proper place in the mind of the Christian, and suffering keeps the Christian from putting too much hope in this world and from getting too attached to worldly things. This mindset helps them live righteously. Likewise, the knowledge that the Christian's time on earth is temporary, like the nation of Israel in exile, leads Christians to practice self-control, care for others, and serve God. Peter concludes with a reminder that suffering for a crime is justice, but suffering for Jesus' sake, though difficult, is a blessing.

Peter ends his letter in Chapter 5 with an exhortation to spiritual leaders to lead well, especially during difficult times. Christian elders are to act like shepherds, caring for the people under their sphere of influence. Christian elders should also be willing servants and not greedy or desirous of power. They are to lead by example, live humbly, be watchful, and rest in the knowledge that Jesus will return to fix the world once and for all.

KEY TAKEAWAYS

Peter wants his readers to take great comfort in the fact that suffering and injustice are not forever, but at times they must be endured. This suffering is not a sign of God's disapproval; Christians face what Jesus faced. Peter calls his readers to live righteously as a testimony to the grace of God, especially in the midst of suffering and persecution, and to keep their eyes fixed on the return of Jesus as their ultimate salvation.

2 PETER AND JUDE

A Condemnation of False Teaching

"It was needful for me to write unto you, and exhort you that ye should earnestly contend for the faith which was once delivered unto the saints."
—Jude 3

Jude and 2 Peter do not sit side by side in the New Testament, but both of these short letters were written to help combat false teaching. Though a decade or more might separate them, both letters are a call to great vigilance when it comes to soundly teaching the Christian faith and correcting false teaching.

A PAIR OF LETTERS
ABOUT FALSE TEACHING

The letter of 2 Peter bears the name of Simon Peter as its author and is traditionally believed to have been written by Peter the Apostle. This puts the traditional date for 2 Peter before Peter's death in the mid- to late A.D. 60s. It is also quite likely that 2 Peter is literarily dependent upon Jude as a source for at least some of its content, so the letter was written after Jude. There is nothing in the letter to indicate the location of the recipients, but if it was a companion letter to 1 Peter, then it was written to churches in Asia Minor as 1 Peter was.

Who Was in Jesus' Immediate Family?

Most people know that Mary and Joseph were Jesus' earthly parents, and the New Testament authors James and Jude are traditionally identified as Jesus' brothers. The Gospels also name Simon and Joses as his brothers (e.g., Mark 6:3) and make several references to his "sisters," though they are not named.

Likewise, Jude (*Judas* in Greek) identifies its author in the first verse as "Jude, the servant of Jesus Christ, and brother of James." Traditionally, James here has been identified as the son of Mary and Joseph and thus the brother of Jesus. The letter itself contains few clues as to the date of its production beyond naming the author, but most scholars who take the letter's own claim of authorship seriously date the letter to before A.D. 70. The letter does not divulge its provenance or the location of its recipients.

PETER WARNS THE CHURCHES

The false teachers in 2 Peter are described as those who ultimately deny Jesus. Their teachings are sensual and blasphemous. They speak lofty things about the heavenly realm, though what they say is irrational, and they deny the return of Jesus at the end of the world.

The first wave of false teaching during the New Testament era was the Judaizing heresy, a false teaching that was Jewish in origin and condemned in Galatians and at the Council of Jerusalem (Acts 15). The second wave of false teaching was Greek in origin. Often centered in Asia Minor (Turkey), this second wave was what would become full-blown Christian Gnosticism in the second century. It is likely this second wave of false teaching that gives rise to Peter's letter of warning.

The Foundations of Christianity

Peter organizes his letter into three broad sections. In Chapter 1, he reminds his readers that spiritual maturity and practiced obedience to the Scriptures are the keys to living successfully in this world. He also reminds his readers that Christianity is not some "cunningly devised" myth but rather is based on the teaching of Jesus as witnessed by those who knew him. These witnesses are still alive in Peter's day to confirm what they saw and heard. This eyewitness testimony, recorded in the Scripture, is "a more sure word of prophecy" than the Greek myths and legends (2 Peter 1:16–21).

The Dangers of False Teachers

Chapter 2 of 2 Peter is concerned with the false teachers themselves. Peter gives some details on their beliefs but mostly focuses on how their theological error leads to unrighteous living. Beliefs always lead to actions, and false beliefs lead to destructive actions. Peter compares these false teachers with wicked people who fell under God's judgment in the Old Testament. He also warns that though these false teachers are not always easy to spot at first, they are always looking for new converts to their errors. The fact that they know the truth but have turned from it will make them all the more culpable in the day of judgment.

In Chapter 3, Peter takes on a specific belief of these false teachers: their denial that Jesus, God's Messiah, will one day return to judge the world. Peter reminds his readers that God spoke and created the world, and God spoke and destroyed the world with a flood in Noah's day. God has also spoken and promised the return of Jesus to judge the world, and God is always as good as His word. God has delayed the coming of Jesus, Peter argues, because He is delaying his judgment so that more people will have a chance to repent and be saved. But He will not delay forever.

JUDE CONTENDS FOR THE FAITH

Though it is only twenty-five verses, Jude is packed with powerful and convincing language. Like 2 Peter, Jude encourages his readers to achieve spiritual maturity and to "contend for the faith" (Jude 1:3) with sound teaching. He warns of false teachers who are already inside the church, leading people astray. Also, like 2 Peter, Jude compares these false teachers with people in the Old Testament who fell under God's judgment for abandoning the truth. Jude also makes clear that incorrect beliefs lead to destructive behavior, and these false teachers have very destructive behavior indeed. Jude ends his letter with a reminder that Christians are to build themselves up in the faith and to rescue those who are being duped by false teaching.

KEY TAKEAWAYS

Both Jude and 2 Peter issue clear exhortations to Christians everywhere to be sure that they know the truth from the Scripture and teach it correctly to others. Corruptions of the gospel are everywhere, and it is the duty of the people of God to combat false teaching with sound teaching at every opportunity.

1–3 JOHN

Letters to Churches Struggling with Their Faith

"I have not written unto you because ye know not the truth, but because ye know it, and that no lie is of the truth."
—1 John 2:21

The letters of John are written to a confused and hurting collection of churches that has gone through a schism over competing understandings of Jesus. John writes these Christians three letters—one to all the churches in the area, one to a specific church, and one to a leader in one of those churches—to encourage them to understand that they have believed in the real Jesus and to help them continue the mission of Jesus.

A SCHISM AMONG THE CHURCHES

The three letters of John were ultimately added to the New Testament under the belief that they were written by the Apostle John. Because of similarity of language between the Gospel of John and these letters, 1-3 John are generally dated to around A.D. 90, though scholars who hold to a different author for 1-3 John have a wide variety of dates for the letters. John is traditionally associated with the city of Ephesus in western Asia Minor (Turkey), so the letters were likely written to Christian churches in and around Ephesus. The letters of John tell a singular story and were apparently written shortly after a huge theological rift happened in the churches that tore them in two.

THREE LETTERS, ONE STORY

The schism came about as the result of a group of false teachers who were teaching a different version of Jesus. "They went out from us, but they were not of us," John writes (1 John 2:19). Though the exact nature of this false teaching is unknown, John says that they denied that "Jesus is the Christ" (1 John 2:22), and they did not confess that "Jesus Christ is come in the flesh" (1 John 4:2). They also apparently claimed that it was possible to become sinless though they taught sinful practices, and they brought with them hatred and strife.

The schism left the members of these churches hurting, confused, and wondering if they had believed in the real Jesus. John writes 1 John to reassure the churches that they believed in the real Jesus and that the departure of the false teachers was a good thing. John writes 2 John to encourage a particular church to use care in whom it receives and sends as missionaries in the aftermath of the schism. Finally, John writes 3 John as a letter of recommendation for a missionary, so they will know he is not one of the false teachers, and to rebuke a Christian for frustrating that church's missionary efforts.

THAT THEY MAY KNOW THEY HAVE ETERNAL LIFE

The letter of 1 John is divided into five chapters, but it is organized around three tests. John wants to reassure the Christian churches that they, unlike the false teachers whom he calls "antichrists," have believed in the real Jesus. John gives them the three tests and assures them that they pass with flying colors.

John's first test is belief that Jesus was the Messiah who was God come in the flesh. The false teachers denied this essential truth, but the Christians he is writing to affirmed it. This test first appears in Chapter 1, and then John circles back to it in Chapter 4. Anyone can claim anything about Jesus' identity, but John actually knew Jesus. The Apostolic witness, John argues, is the only reliable witness to the true identity of Jesus.

The second test—striving to follow Jesus in living righteously—is also introduced in Chapter 1 and is the focus of Chapters 2 and 3. The false teachers apparently taught ethics that were contrary to the teaching of Jesus and encouraged unrighteous living.

John's third test is one of love. True followers of Jesus love one another, but these false teachers brought with them hatred and dissension.

John ends his letter with more reassurance: "These things have I written unto you that believe on the name of the Son of God; that ye may know that ye have eternal life" (1 John 5:13). The differences between Jesus' true followers and the false teachers are obvious. John wants to be sure that these Christians understand that as well.

Antichrist and Antichrists

The term *Antichrist* (*antichristos* in Greek) occurs only in 1 and 2 John in the Bible. John primarily uses the plural, *Antichrists*, to refer to those who have abandoned the Apostolic understanding of Jesus and the gospel, but many Christians use the singular term to describe the end-times figure from Revelation 13.

BEWARE FALSE TEACHERS

John's second letter reads like 1 John in miniature. After a brief introduction, he reiterates the three tests. John, however, has an additional purpose in mind. The false teachers are continuing to do missionary work throughout Asia Minor. John explains that these false teachers have gone out of the church and into the world as missionaries for their false teaching. The true followers of Jesus must be sure that in their zeal to send and support missionaries, they do not support one of these false teachers. If they do not pass the three tests, Christians should not receive a teacher into their houses (churches) or give them public recognition or support.

A LETTER OF RECOMMENDATION

John's trio of letters ends with a letter of recommendation written to Gaius, a leader in one of the churches that John knows. John is commending a man, probably a missionary, named Demetrius to the church, so they will know that he is a true follower of Jesus and not one of the false teachers. In the letter, John also condemns Diotrephes, who has used the occasion of the false teaching and the split to put himself in charge and is refusing to send or receive *any* missionaries. John mentions him only briefly and then promises a visit soon in which he will help deal with Diotrephes.

KEY TAKEAWAYS

Belief that Jesus was the Christ who was God in the flesh, striving to live righteously according to the teaching of Jesus, and love for one another are the hallmarks of the Christian faith. Those who live out the faith of Jesus "knoweth God" (1 John 4:7). For John, that is the greatest assurance of all, and these are the messages he focuses on in these chapters.

REVELATION

A Literary Apocalypse

> "And God shall wipe away all tears from their eyes; and there shall
> be no more death, neither sorrow, nor crying, neither shall there be
> any more pain: for the former things are passed away."
> —Revelation 21:4

Apocalyptic beliefs about the end of the world are common in every culture, both religious and secular. The book of Revelation is a literary apocalypse, written to seven churches in Asia Minor, detailing four visions about how God plans to ultimately rescue his people and bring justice and righteousness to the creation by ending this world and establishing a better world in its place: the Kingdom of God.

THE VISION OF THE APOSTLE JOHN

The author of Revelation identifies himself as "John," and Revelation was added to Christian Scripture under the widespread belief that this John was the Apostle. Some ancient Christians and many modern scholars, however, have produced other theories as to the identity of the author and as to how the text of Revelation relates to the Gospel of John and 1–3 John. Regardless, it is generally believed that Revelation was written near the end of the first century, apparently from Patmos, an island about sixty miles off the coast of Ephesus.

UNDERSTANDING AN APOCALYPSE

Christians throughout the centuries have developed many theological models for understanding Revelation. Most of these theories, for most of Christian history, have understood Revelation to be about the coming of the Kingdom of God, which is, in at least some sense, still in the future. Revelation then recounts God's activity in the past, speaks about the current suffering of the book's original audience, and makes promises about God's future return and rescue.

Did John Invent the Apocalypse?

John did not invent the apocalypse just as Jesus did not invent the parable. The apocalyptic literary form—texts, frequently about the end of the world, which include visions, dreams, heavy symbolism, and divine revelation—had existed for centuries prior to Revelation. John fashions his visions into a pre-existing literary form, following patterns laid out primarily in the Old Testament, especially in the book of Daniel.

Revelation is written to encourage Christians living through difficult times, and to reassure them that the suffering and persecution of Jesus' followers will not go on forever. God will one day radically intervene to bring the world to an end, judge the wicked, and establish the Kingdom of God. Revelation is not, therefore, primarily a warning. Rather, it is a promise, that this world as it is now, with all its evil and suffering, will not endure. Evil will be overthrown. Goodness will reign because God Himself, in the person of Jesus, will reign.

THE FIRST VISION:
THE DRAMA OF THE END

The first vision in Revelation 1–3 is a vision of Christ himself. Jesus appears to John in a highly symbolic form and instructs John to write letters from Jesus to seven churches in cities in Asia Minor. With few exceptions, each of these short letters accomplishes three things:

1. They compliment the church on how well they are following Jesus.
2. They offer some sort of critique for what the churches are getting wrong.
3. They make a symbolic promise with language that is related to the language about the end of the world.

Symbolism in Revelation

The imagery and symbolism in Revelation are borrowed almost entirely from the Old Testament. When readers encounter a symbolic depiction in Revelation, their first question should be "When this image occurs in the Old Testament, what does it mean there?" That is likely the meaning that John intends as well. For example, in Revelation 12, when John describes the image of a child who will "rule all nations with a rod of iron" (Revelation 12:5) he is symbolizing the Messiah who is described in the Old Testament with that language.

THE SECOND VISION:
JUDGMENT AND SALVATION

The second vision takes up more than half of the book of Revelation. In Revelation 4–5, John witnesses a heavenly scene in which Jesus is symbolically depicted as a lamb that was slain and has returned to life. In Revelation 6–8, John witnesses a seven-sealed scroll opened, one seal at a time. With the breaking of each seal, God pours out His judgment upon the wicked on the earth. John witnesses seven angels blowing seven trumpets in Revelation 9–11, one after the other, and with the blowing of these trumpets God brings more judgments for sin upon the earth. In both of these series of judgments, John sees glimpses of God's rescue and His coming kingdom.

John's vision breaks from declarations of judgment in Revelation 12–15 when John sees a number of supernatural entities, some of whom are displayed in highly symbolic form. Though there is little agreement among scholars as to the exact meaning of these symbols, John appears to be using these entities to tell the story of salvation history. The Messiah is born into the nation of Israel. Satan, the dragon, tries to destroy God incarnate but fails. Satan is defeated, and now that Satan knows his days are numbered, he tries to bring as much death and destruction to the earth as he can. The final two entities, the beast out of the sea and the beast out of the earth, are symbolic representations of the working of evil on the planet as God's people await the arrival of God and His Kingdom.

The second vision ends with a depiction of seven angels in Revelation 15–16. Each of these angels holds a bowl containing the wrath of God, and one by one, they pour out that wrath upon the earth.

THE THIRD VISION:
A NEW HEAVEN AND EARTH

John's third vision in Revelation 17–20 depicts God's final victory over evil in the world. All of the world's evils—governmental evil, spiritual and religious evil, economic evil—are depicted as Babylon, the enemy of Israel in the Old Testament, and all these evils are destroyed by God. The vision ends with the coming of Christ, his judgment of the world, and his reign in the Kingdom of God. Only those who have believed the gospel, who are found "written in the book of life," enter into God's Kingdom (Revelation 20:12, 15).

The final vision in Revelation 21–22 is a vision of a new heaven and a new earth. The return of God in the person of Christ is not just for rescue and judgment. Christ will fix the world that humans have wrecked. The imagery in these final two chapters is primarily images of relief, rest, healing, and goodness. When God dwells with His people, they are not sick. They do not weep. They do not hurt themselves or others anymore. They will see God's face, and He will put his name on them. This is the world that ultimately awaits God's people.

KEY TAKEAWAYS

John ends his apocalypse with a promise and a warning. The promise is that Jesus will return; the words of Revelation are true. The warning is to take heed and to wait faithfully.

THE BIBLE TODAY

The Influence of This Monumental Work

"And this gospel of the kingdom shall be preached
in all the world for a witness unto all nations."
—Matthew 24:14

It is not controversial to say that the Bible is one of the most influential books in the history of the world. Christianity is still the majority religion on planet Earth, and 2.3 billion people believe the Bible to be their sacred Scripture. It is likely that the influence of the Bible will continue far into the future.

BIBLE TRANSLATION WORK

Over the centuries, the Bible has been translated into many different languages. The Hebrew Old Testament was translated into Aramaic and Greek very early, and by the fourth century, the New Testament had been translated into Latin, Coptic, Syriac, and many other languages. Today the Bible exists in more than seven hundred languages, giving almost six billion people access to the Bible in their native tongue.

MODERN ENGLISH TRANSLATIONS

To date, the full Bible has been translated into English in well over one hundred different versions. Are that many different translations really necessary? It is a good question.

Novel Translations

Produced for their novelty, not their usefulness, a number of unusual translations of the Bible into English are currently available: *Bible Emoji: Scripture 4 Millennials*, *The Bible in Cockney*, and *The Phat News of Mark* (a translation for "hippies") are just a few. The Bible has even been translated into Klingon.

There is still great demand for Bibles in the world, and in the world of modern publishing, Bible production is a lucrative business. Many of the older English translations have been revised and updated with more modern English, especially those whose translations have passed into the public domain and thus can be altered and reprinted without copyright infringement. And English is still an ever-changing language. Scholars constantly want to update English translations so they can be as accurate to the original as they can be in modern English. There are many modern, fresh translations of the ancient Greek and Hebrew texts of the Bible. They are more accurate, more transparent, and more scholarly than translations have ever been. When it comes to the Bible, the English speaker truly has an embarrassment of riches.

THE BIBLE AND TECHNOLOGY

Technology has dramatically increased access to the Bible around the world and made Bible study simpler and easier. There are numerous popular Bible apps that aggregate the many English translations of the Bible into a single place as well as provide access to translations of the Bible in other languages. The most popular Bible apps contain more than 2,000 different translations in more than 1,200 different languages. These Bible apps also allow users to highlight, bookmark, and take notes right in the app.

There are also many Bible study websites and paid software packages that host the vast majority of English translations as well as the texts of the ancient Greek and Hebrew manuscripts from which those translations were made. With one click, students of the Bible can see a Bible word in the original language with the definition of that word from scholarly sources as well as how that word was translated from the seventeenth-century King James to every modern translation. These websites and software packages also typically host other translation and theological resources as well as devotional material and other Bible study aids.

KEY TAKEAWAYS

It would be impossible to overestimate the influence of the Bible on the world today. It is a comprehensive guide to knowing God and knowing His Son, Jesus Christ, and informs the lives of more people than any other religious text.

INDEX

1 Chronicles, 31, 131–32, 134, 175–78

1 Corinthians, 179, 181, 210, 212–13, 220–23, 252

1 John, 179, 181, 269–74

1 Kings, 29, 91–96

1 Peter, 179, 181, 261–65

1 Samuel, 10, 29, 71, 83–86

1 Thessalonians, 179, 212, 241–44

1 Timothy, 179, 213, 245–48

2 Chronicles, 31, 131–32, 134, 175–78

2 Corinthians, 179, 181, 212, 220–24

2 John, 179, 181, 269–74

2 Kings, 29, 71, 91, 96–100, 178

2 Peter, 179, 181, 265–68

2 Samuel, 10, 22, 29, 69–70, 72, 87–91, 134, 137, 176, 192

2 Thessalonians, 179, 212, 241–44

2 Timothy, 14, 179, 214, 245–48

3 John, 179, 181, 269–74

Abraham
    family of, 21–22, 35, 40–45, 63, 190
    promise to, 35, 50–53, 59–60, 67–69, 76, 92, 123, 133, 170, 177
    "seed" of, 22, 35, 63

Acts, 22, 179–80, 198, 206–12, 215, 225, 230, 234, 238, 241, 259, 266

Adam, 11, 21, 34–39, 58, 69, 114, 131, 134, 151, 156, 200

Ahab, 94–97

Amos, 30, 116, 118–20

Antichrists, 270–71

Apocalyptic literature, 179–81, 192, 274–78

Apocalyptic visions, 161–65

Apocrypha, 12, 212

Ark of the Covenant, 53, 74, 84, 87–88, 90, 113, 176

Balaam, 63, 158

Benjamin, 43–45, 62, 81–85, 158, 176

Bible. *See also specific books*
    apps for, 280–81
    beliefs about, 11–13, 184, 237–40, 279
    books of, 10–19, 27–28, 32–36, 179–81
    chapters of, 17–19
    explanation of, 7–13
    footnotes in, 14, 18–19
    headings in, 14, 18–19
    history of, 14–16
    influence of, 279–81
    language of, 14–19, 26
    marginal notes in, 14, 18–19
    meaning of, 10–13
    modern Bible, 10–19, 179–83, 188, 224, 279–81
    organization of, 14–19, 25–31, 179–81
    origin of, 10
    as Scripture, 9–13, 20–24, 183, 210, 279–80
    study of, 12, 18–19, 280–81
    technology and, 280–81
    translations of, 14–16, 21, 26–27, 279–81
    verses of, 17–19
    versions of, 15–18, 27–28, 279–81

Books of Bible. *See also specific books*
  abbreviations of, 16–17
  chapters of, 17–19
  footnotes in, 14, 18–19
  headings in, 14, 18–19
  marginal notes in, 14, 18–19
  organization of, 14–19, 25–31, 179–81
  overview of, 10–19, 27–28, 32–36
  verses of, 17–19
Burning bush, 47, 147, 203

Cherubim, 39, 53, 111–13
Christian church, 206–7, 220–23, 247, 252, 257, 269–71
Christianity
  beliefs of, 12–13, 184, 237–40, 279
  doctrines of, 215–19, 241–44
  foundations of, 267
  handbook for, 237–40
  spread of, 180, 207–9, 215–19
  truths of, 229–32
Cleanliness laws, 56–58
Colossians, 179, 212, 237–40, 249
Creation, 37–38, 154, 195, 267
Cyrus, 132, 134, 162, 166–67, 175, 178

Daniel, 26, 31, 131, 134, 161–65, 173, 275
David, 21–22, 69–72, 83, 85–120, 125–38, 144–52, 156, 160–65, 175–78
Day of Atonement, 58–59
Day of the LORD, 72, 116, 118–21, 124–26, 129–30, 133
Dead Sea Scrolls, 27
Deuterocanonical books, 12
Deuteronomy, 29, 32–33, 65–68, 72, 101, 106, 119, 170, 172

Divine wisdom, 57, 92, 131–34, 139–48, 153, 177, 258–60

Ecclesiastes, 30, 131, 133–34, 153–56
Elihu, 139, 142
Elijah, 94–97, 100, 129
Ephesians, 179, 212, 229–32, 237, 240
Erotic love poem, 133, 149, 151–52
Esther, 31, 131, 133–34, 157–60
Eve, 11, 21, 34, 38–39, 58, 69, 114, 145, 151–52
Exodus, 29, 32–33, 46–55, 66, 129, 203
Exodus 1–18, 46–50
Exodus 19–40, 51–55
Ezekiel, 30, 72, 111–15
Ezra, 26, 31, 131–32, 134, 166–70, 172–75

Fall/fallen world, 38–40, 151–53, 156
False teachers, 209, 223–26, 234–35, 238, 246, 265–68, 270–72
Flood, 11, 39–40, 124, 267–68

Galatians, 179, 211–12, 224–28, 238, 266
Genesis, 25, 29, 32–33, 37–45, 56–59, 112, 153, 156–57, 159, 195, 217, 227
Genesis 1–11, 37–40
Genesis 12–50, 41–45
God
  as Creator, 37–38, 154, 195, 267
  meaning of name, 47
  Messenger of, 52–54, 113, 126–30
  miracles of, 46, 49–50, 73, 96–97, 163
  plagues from, 47–50, 62, 84
  Son of, 138, 148, 184–86, 192–97, 202–5, 211, 223, 254, 271, 281

wisdom of, 57, 92, 131–34, 139–48, 153, 177, 258–60

word of, 12–13, 34–40, 46–55, 65–68, 78–86, 93, 98, 102–22, 138–47, 165–74, 203, 243, 255

Golden calf, 53–55, 67, 129

Gomorrah, 41–42, 78

Gospels

explanation of, 13, 179–88

four Gospels, 13, 17–19, 179–205

of Jesus, 184–85, 195, 199–201, 207, 215–19, 221

of New Testament, 13, 17–19, 179–205

order of, 199

spelling of, 184–85

synoptic question and, 187–88

Great Commission, 209, 215

Habakkuk, 30, 121, 124–25

Haggai, 30, 126–27, 130, 166–67, 169

Hannah, 83–84

Hebrew poetry, 136

Hebrews, 179, 181, 253–56

Herodians, 205

Hezekiah, 96–104, 147, 178

Holiness laws, 56, 59–60

Hosea, 30, 116–17, 120

"I am" statements, 203–5

Idols/idolatry, 52–54, 59, 66–77, 80–82, 84, 93–99, 107–11, 113–19, 125–29, 154, 217

Immanuel, 101–5

Intermarriage, 96, 166, 169

Isaac, 21–22, 35, 41–43, 56, 69, 177–78

Isaiah, 19, 29, 72, 97–98, 101–5

Jacob, 21–22, 35, 41–46, 61–62, 69, 119–20, 157, 257

James, 179, 257–60, 266

Jeremiah, 29, 72, 106–10, 164, 166, 178

Jesus

baptism of, 184, 190, 196, 200

belief about Bible, 11, 13

birth of, 181, 184, 186–87, 190, 195–96, 199, 203

crucifixion of, 197, 228, 256

death of, 180–82, 189–93, 197–98, 201, 203–5, 207–8, 227–28, 243, 256

disciples of, 9, 22, 180, 186–87, 191–97, 200–205, 209, 226

execution of, 193, 197, 201, 203, 228, 256

eyewitness accounts of, 185–88, 195, 267

faithfulness to, 230, 247–48, 253–56

final days of, 189–93, 197, 201, 203

gospel of, 184–85, 195, 199–201, 207, 215–19, 221

life of, 184–92, 195–203, 213

ministry of, 18, 184–92, 195–203

miracles of, 185, 189, 191–93, 195–97, 200–205, 207–8

parables of, 186, 191–92, 199–201, 275

parents of, 186–87, 193, 199–200, 266

resurrection of, 22, 180, 182, 185, 189–93, 197, 201, 203–5, 222, 227, 243, 256

as Savior, 22, 104, 184–86, 189, 193–94, 197–200, 205, 210, 217–18, 232, 239

sermons of, 189–93, 196

as Son of God, 184–86, 192–97, 202–5, 211, 223, 254, 271, 281
travel narrative of, 200–201

Job, 30, 131–34, 139–43

Joel, 22, 30, 116–18, 120, 125

John, 20, 179–81, 184, 190, 196, 199–200, 202–5, 269–72, 274–78

John the Baptist, 190, 196

Jonah, 11, 30, 121–22, 125, 201

Joseph, 35, 43–46, 62, 133–34, 160–61, 266

Joshua, 29, 62, 64–65, 68, 70, 73–78, 100, 126–27, 166–67, 172, 254–55

Josiah, 96–100, 178

Jude, 18, 179, 265–68

Judges, 29, 70–71, 78–82, 150

King James Version (KJV), 15–16, 114, 230, 281

Lady Folly, 144–46

Lady Wisdom, 144–46, 148, 151–52

Lamentations, 31, 131, 133–34, 153, 155–56

Law, 9–11, 28, 31–33, 36, 56–61, 64–67. *See also* Torah

Lazarus, 203–4

Leviticus, 29, 32–33, 56–60

Luke, 179–80, 184, 186–87, 193, 195, 198–202, 206–11

Malachi, 19, 30, 72, 126, 128–30

Mark, 19, 179–81, 184, 187, 189, 194–97, 199–202, 266, 280

Mary, 186–87, 193, 199, 266

Mary Magdalene, 193

Masoretic Text, 27

Matthew, 13, 17–18, 179–80, 184–93, 195–96, 199–202, 243, 279

Messenger of God, 52–54, 113, 126–30

Micah, 30, 81, 121, 123, 125

Miracles, 46, 49–50, 73, 96–97, 163, 185, 189, 191–93, 195–97, 200–205, 207–8

Mosaic Covenant, 24, 33, 53, 67

Moses
    birth of, 46–47
    book of, 28, 98–101, 137, 167
    commandments of, 52–54, 66, 84
    death of, 68, 70, 73
    as God's servant, 46–58, 77, 254–55
    laws of, 24, 33, 52–54, 66–68, 84, 92–94, 161
    as prophet, 21–22, 35–36, 62–70, 94, 98–101, 129, 158–61
    sermons of, 106

Mount Sinai, 32–36, 46–55, 61–63, 65–66, 68, 75, 94, 122, 129, 151

Nahum, 30, 121, 123–25

Nebuchadnezzar, 99–100, 109, 161–63

Nehemiah, 31, 131–32, 134, 170–74

New Testament
    basics of, 179–83
    books in, 10, 12–13, 17–19, 180–83, 214
    copies of, 182–83
    date of, 181–82
    explanation of, 9–13, 20–24
    foundation of, 21–22
    Gospels of, 13, 17–19, 179–205
    layout of, 179–81
    manuscripts of, 182–83
    Old Testament and, 9–13, 20–24

origins of, 181–83
as Scripture, 9–13, 20–24, 183, 210
translations of, 279–80
views on, 9–13, 20–24
Noah, 11, 34, 39–40, 93, 124, 268
Numbers, 29, 32–33, 61–64, 66

Obadiah, 30, 116, 119–20
Old Testament
basics of, 25–31
books in, 10, 12–13, 17–19, 27–31
explanation of, 9–13, 20–36
as foundation, 21–22
languages of, 26
manuscripts of, 26–27
New Testament and, 9–13, 20–24
order of, 25–31
prophets of, 9–11, 21–31, 35–38, 62–72, 98–101, 116–30, 158–61
review of, 175–78
as Scripture, 9–13, 20–24
Torah and, 24–36
translations of, 21, 26–27, 279–80
views on, 9–13, 20–24
Onesimus, 249–52

Parables, 186, 191–92, 199–201, 275
Paul
beginnings of, 210–11
birth of, 210–11
death of, 211, 213, 246–48
final days of, 212–13, 245–48, 259
letters of, 179–81, 210–53
travels of, 210–14, 236, 241–42
Pentateuch, 32. See also Torah
Peter the Apostle, 22, 180, 194–96, 207–8, 226, 261–62, 265
Pharisees, 26, 205

Philemon, 179, 212, 249–52
Philippians, 179, 212, 233–36
Plagues, 47–50, 62, 84
Prophets
as book, 69–70
Former Prophets, 29, 69–72
Latter Prophets, 29–30, 69–72
of Old Testament, 9–11, 21–31, 35–38, 62–72, 98–101, 116–30, 158–61
overview of, 69–72
twelve minor prophets, 29–30, 69, 116–30
Proverbs, 30, 71, 131, 133–34, 144–52
Psalms, 9, 22, 30, 131–38

Red Sea, 46, 49–50, 68, 74
Revelation, 179, 181, 271, 274–78
Romans, 17, 179, 212–13, 215–19, 230
Ruth, 30, 71, 131, 133–34, 149–52, 169

Sacrifice laws, 56–57, 59–60
Sadducees, 205
Salvation, 105–7, 117, 122–28, 137–38, 184, 205–9, 215–19, 224–35, 247, 264, 277
Saul, 70–71, 83–89, 158–60, 176, 207–11
Scripture
Bible as, 9–13, 20–24, 183, 210, 279–80
New Testament as, 9–13, 20–24, 183, 210
obedience to, 191, 257–59, 267–68
Old Testament as, 9–13, 20–24
"Seed" imagery, 22, 34–35, 39–45, 53, 59, 63, 68
Septuagint, 27
Sermon on the Mount, 191
Seven signs, 203–4

Sin
  confessing, 48, 59, 75, 166,
    169–70, 173
  continual sin, 34, 54, 61–62, 78–
    93, 95, 119–21, 155–56, 174–75
  egregious sin, 78, 84, 91, 95
  forgiveness of, 67, 108, 123, 195,
    200, 217–18, 222, 255
  laws for, 56–60
  repentance of, 38–40, 56–60,
    89–95, 99–108, 116–22, 127–29,
    136–45, 163, 166, 169–74, 185,
    190–92, 195–97, 201
  sexual sin, 41–42, 59, 81, 217, 220–22
  spread of, 39–42, 78, 82
Slavery, 249–52, 255
Sodom, 41–42, 67, 78, 82
Solomon, 30, 70–71, 89, 91–95, 100,
  115, 127, 131, 133–34, 137, 144–55,
  167, 174–78
Song of Solomon (Song of Songs),
  30, 131, 133–34, 149, 151–52
Son of David, 22, 69–72, 87–92, 95–
  99, 101–7, 114–20, 125–38, 144–52,
  156, 160–65, 175–78
Son of God, 138, 148, 184–86, 192–97,
  202–5, 211, 223, 254, 271, 281
Son of Man, 161–65, 198
Suffering Servant, 104–5, 197

Tabernacle, 51–53, 55–59, 61, 71, 81,
  83, 86, 107, 128, 176, 255
Tanakh, 9–10, 13, 25
Ten Commandments, 52–54, 66, 84
Theophilus, 199–201, 206
Titus, 179, 212–13, 226, 245–48
Torah
  as book, 65–72

characters in, 34–36
explanation of, 9, 24–36
genealogy and, 28–32, 36, 39–40,
  175–76
genres of, 32–33
law codes of, 9–11, 28, 31–33,
  36, 56–61, 64–67, 161, 166, 169,
  171–73, 191, 225–27
Old Testament and, 24–36
overview of, 32–36
rejecting, 82, 124
remembering, 126–34, 157–60
Translations
  of Bible, 14–16, 21, 26–27, 279–81
  of New Testament, 279–80
  of Old Testament, 21, 26–27,
    279–80
  unusual translations, 280
Tree of life, 39, 112, 145, 163
Twelve Minor Prophets, 29–30, 69,
  116–30

Wilderness, 50, 61–65, 86, 90, 104,
  188, 200, 255
Writings
  as book, 131–32
  confession in, 169, 173
  explanation of, 9–11, 25, 30–31,
    131–34
  of Old Testament, 9–11, 24–25,
    28, 30–31, 131–34
  order of, 131–32
  overview of, 131–34

Zechariah, 30, 126–28, 130, 166–67,
  169
Zephaniah, 30, 121, 124–25

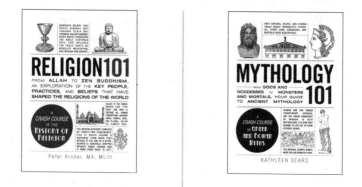